Patricia and Robert Foulke, enthusiastic sailors, hikers, cyclists, and skiiers, have spent four years during the past twenty-five living and traveling in Europe as a couple, with children and adults from 3 to 90 years old.

Patricia Foulke is a remedial reading teacher in Glens Falls, New York. She has a B.A. and an M.A. from the University of Minnesota and from Trinity College and is a doctoral candidate at SUNY-Albany. She has taught for eighteen years and has lectured and written articles on reading and language development.

Robert Foulke is chairman of the English Department at Skidmore College. With a B.A. from Princeton and a Ph.D. from the University of Minnesota, he has taught at Minnesota, Trinity College (Hartford), and Skidmore. He has published a textbook and has lectured and written on literary theory, the English curriculum, Joseph Conrad, maritime history, and sea literature.

Patricia and Robert Foulke

EUROPE UNDER CANVAS

A Guide to Camping for Singles, Couples, or Families

Prentice-Hall, Inc. A SPECTRUM BOOK Englewood Cliffs, N.J.

Library of Congress Cataloging in Publication Data

Foulke, Patricia.
    Europe under canvas.

    (A Spectrum Book)
    Includes index.
    1. Camping—Europe.   2. Europe—Description and
travel—1971–   —Guide-books.   I. Foulke, Robert,
joint author.   II. Title.
GV191.48.E8F68   647′.944   79–22155
ISBN 0–13–292094–8
ISBN 0–13–292086–7 pbk.

Editorial production/supervision
and interior design by Heath Silberfeld
Manufacturing buyer: Barbara A. Frick
Cover © 1979 by Judith Kazdym Leeds

A SPECTRUM BOOK

Printed in the United States of America

10 9 8 7 6 5 4 3 2 1

PRENTICE-HALL INTERNATIONAL, INC., London
PRENTICE-HALL OF AUSTRALIA PTY. LIMITED, Sydney
PRENTICE-HALL OF CANADA, LTD., Toronto
PRENTICE-HALL OF INDIA PRIVATE LIMITED, New Delhi
PRENTICE-HALL OF JAPAN, INC., Tokyo
PRENTICE-HALL OF SOUTHEAST ASIA PTE. LTD., Singapore
WHITEHALL BOOKS LIMITED, Wellington, New Zealand

contents

1
introduction 1

AN OVERVIEW 2
Why camp? 2, The Book We Longed for—and Couldn't
Find 3, Lessons Learned in Camping Travel Over 25
Years 4

2
planning 7

DECIDING 8
Anticipation 8, Planning Your Route 9, Estimating Your
Expenses and Getting Money 11, Purchasing
Insurance 13, Passports and Customs 14
GETTING THERE 14
Choosing Your Airfare 14, Finding a Ship 16
COLLECTING 18
Clothing 18, Packing 21, Camping Equipment 22,
Equipment for Children 28, Tourist Information 28

COUNTDOWN FOR CAMPERS   31

HOUSEHOLDING   32

Selecting a Base for Longer Stays   32, Choosing and Timing Your Trips   35

FINDING THE RIGHT TRANSPORTATION   36

Automobile Rental, Lease, or Purchase   36, Caravan Rental   38, Car Shipment Home   39, Ferry Transportation   39

3

coping   40

FINDING GOOD CAMPSITES   41

Location   42, Desirable Amenities   43, Seasons and Holidays   43, Campsite Guides   44

EATING   45

Campsite Cooking   46, Local Wines and Beers   46, Cooking by Computer   47, Sample Menu Plans for One Week   48, Dinner Recipes   50

PAYING   62

Comparative Food Costs   62, Avoiding Campsite Inflation   64, How to Keep Money in Your Pocket   66

GETTING HELP WHEN YOU NEED IT   67

Getting Bumped from a Flight   68, Losing Your Passport   68, Losing Your Traveler's Checks   68, Resolving Medical Problems   69, Encountering the Law   69

ENJOYING   70

With Children   70, Collecting   71, Keeping a Journal   71, Balancing Tourism and Sports   72, Choosing What to Do   72, Finding Local Sights   72

RELAXING   73

Time Out for Everyone   73, Discovering a Mediterranean Sense of Time   74

4
suggested itineraries   75

THE SOUTHWESTERN CIRCUIT (ENGLAND)   77
THE CENTRAL CIRCUIT (ENGLAND AND WALES)   89
SCOTLAND   104
SCANDINAVIA   114
CENTRAL EUROPE   130
RELATED EXPEDITIONS   157
*Skiing   157, Biking   159, Backpacking   160, Canal
Boating   160*

appendix   163

BOOKS TO READ BEFORE YOU GO   164
LOCAL FOODS TO TRY   165
CONVERSION TABLES   172
*Clothing Size   172, Weights   172, Liquid Measure   172,
Length   172, Distance   172, Gasoline   173,
Temperature   173*

index   173

1

introduction

AN OVERVIEW

Enjoy Europe! Yes, but how can a family, a couple, or a single person enjoying the giddy prospect of a week or a year in Europe make the most of it? Some people prefer to throw things into a suitcase and unravel threads of the trip as they go. Others carefully plan a crammed itinerary that leaves them exhausted and costs a mint. Families hoping to economize can easily spend $100 a day—with guilt mounting as they go. Yet it is possible to travel in Europe without blowing your children's or your own college fund. We discovered that twelve weeks of family camping cost us no more than others spend on a three-week packaged tour.

Why Camp?

There are many reasons for deliberately choosing to camp. Cost is the most obvious one. We know that a family can camp for a fraction of the cost of a hotel trip with all meals out. But there are other advantages as well. Camping can also provide freedom from the meal schedules and dress restrictions of hotels, from constant tips, and railroad timetables. It can let you explore villages and beaches and mountains where there are no hotels, or it can bring you to the periphery of Europe's most interesting cities. People working together making camp, cooking, and relaxing by their tents create a special kind of intimacy. There is a sense of adventure involved in picking a campsite with a gorgeous view in the mountain wilderness, or one with historic interest near an ancient Roman wall or within an old castle enclosure. Camping allows you to travel more while paying less, to be free to live by weather and impulse rather than by one of those intricate itineraries that makes work out of fun.

The Book We Longed for—and Couldn't Find

You need information on camping trips that have been successful. You can make use of some of the information that has been tested by others without losing the zest of your own adventure. You can enjoy the humor of others' mistakes knowing that you will make your own, and discoveries as well. You can save time and effort by remembering to take along the crucial items we didn't think of. You can save the extraordinary amount of time it took us to travel some routes with miserable road conditions we hadn't known about until we endured them. It didn't usually take us more than one trip through a region to learn to allow more time for that 50-mile stretch of curvy, bumpy, narrow roads, but occasionally we had to learn our lesson twice because we were enticed by an equally unknown alternate route. For those who like to explore, lines on a map are irresistible temptations.

Before we started, we searched through many of the travel books on the market and found long lists of hotels, restaurants, sightseeing suggestions, and general information about currency, shopping, and local regulations. But we did not find what we wanted most—information on camping trips actually taken by a family like ours. We wanted to know how much more it would cost to camp in Scandinavia than in England. We wanted to know why camping can be a delight in some areas and a disaster in others. We wanted to hear about what happens, for example, when people innocently choose Easter weekend (one of the busiest weekends of the year in Europe) for an adventure and get trapped in the center of a little Italian town on Good Friday while processions clog all available roads. We wanted to be reassured that camping can be a pleasure again—even after the misery of pitching tents at 1:00 A.M. in a torrential downpour. We wanted to know that gloomy situations could sometimes turn out for the best—like the time a chance encounter with some friendly people late one April night (when campgrounds had not yet opened for the season) led our family to a midnight spread of smørbrod, tenting in our hosts' garden, and a personal tour of Copenhagen the following day. We wanted to know what to do when seemingly impossible barriers were thrown our way—like the time in May we were due to catch a ferry and found that the mountain road leading to it hadn't been plowed!

Lessons Learned in Camping Travel Over 25 Years

We had to discover most of what we needed to know for ourselves while living abroad with our family during four of the last twenty-five years. Having pieced it all together for our own use, we decided to lay it out in a concise guide for people who want to camp in Europe—including singles, couples, and families with children of all ages. The guide begins with a section on planning—deciding where to go in whatever time you have, getting there inexpensively, collecting the necessary equipment and clothing, and selecting a base for longer stays. Realistic estimates of time, distance, and cost will keep you from spoiling your vacation with too much daily rush, and advice on what is essential for camping will help the uninitiated avoid the frustrations of lugging around too much unnecessary gear.

The second section is designed to help you cope effectively with the daily decisions of a camping expedition abroad—driving, finding good campsites, buying and preparing food economically and simply, enjoying sightseeing, getting emergency help if you need it, and relaxing. Reliable sources of information on automobile or camper rental, purchase, or leasing, on ferry schedules and costs, on the purchase or rental of camping equipment, and on how to locate desirable campgrounds will save you time and disappointment. Comparison of the cost of a sample daily menu bought in seven countries illustrates some startling disparities in food prices. Although the fluctuations of the dollar and inflation will make these specific prices vary significantly from year to year, the ratio of comparative food costs is more stable; it helps to be able to plan ahead for travel in countries that are twice as expensive as others. A generous selection of recipes for one- or two-pot meals will help you simplify cooking and keep you from spending too much valuable time on daily chores. Some information on the lifestyle and mores of European campgrounds will smooth the way for you so you can enjoy meeting your European counterparts; this is usually one of the most memorable benefits of a camping venture abroad. The section closes with some advice to harried and hurried Americans—how to relax and avoid the tensions of living in close quarters for extended periods of time.

Planning your itinerary is more difficult when it involves roads and campsites rather than train timetables and hotel reservations. But it is also more satisfying because it can allow for change, for weather, for additions and deletions, for longer or shorter stays based on personal responses to the places visited. A good itinerary for a camping trip compromises between the chaos of wandering around aimlessly and the confinement of sticking to a rigid schedule. Most of all, it should have been tested by someone else, at least in part, so that too many unwanted surprises and miscalculations do not mar the pleasure of your trip. The fourth section of this book contains a selection of itineraries for camping trips that have actually been taken and can be adapted to fit your interests (with details on mileage, routes, sightseeing suggestions, and pleasant locales for base camps). It also includes suggestions on organizing activities that may be combined with a camping trip or undertaken separately—biking, backpacking, canal boating, and skiing. The guide closes with an appendix containing information that most of you may want to refer to frequently while en route.

Instead of groping for camping information and finding only very small portions of it spread here and there in an armful of books, you need only carry this guide, a carefully selected campsite list, one general tour guide, and a few maps. Traveling without a carful of books, pamphlets, and brochures will be more pleasurable and less annoying—particularly for those who are trying to get away from daily lives cluttered with piles of paper awaiting attention.

In addition to these compact sources of most of the information camping families need, you may want to prepare and bring your own notebook for the trip. For years we have clipped articles and saved material that intrigued us. While preparing for a trip we stuff this varied information into a series of file folders, and add notes on what we learn from phone calls or from friends. In the final countdown before the trip, we pare this collection down to essential material and take it along either in Manila envelopes by category or country, or we transcribe it into the notebook. The notebook is handiest: as you travel you may want to write down addresses of new friends, shopping information gleaned from fellow campers to use when you arrive where they have been, recommendations for favorite restaurants, special events in the areas you plan to visit, campgrounds others have enjoyed, and any other special tips you want to remember.

2

planning

DECIDING

Getting the nerve to transform Sunday-afternoon fantasies into airline reservations is the hardest part. Once the choice has been made, you can begin to plan. If you really want to enjoy a camping adventure in Europe, you must be willing to plan as well as dream. Experienced campers tend to be precise and meticulous. The time available will determine the distance that can be covered with pleasure instead of panic. Cost estimates will be realistic only if they include a day-by-day listing of all known expenses and a slush fund for the unexpected opportunities that will crop up and for inflation and fluctuating exchange rates. The focus of the trip—season, sports interests, cultural activities, and the proportion of time spent in large cities or in the country—will determine equipment and clothing needs, destinations, and routes.

Anticipation

Anticipation of a trip abroad is great fun. If you are taking your children, you should share that planning with them—they may not realize what is in store for them. Collecting travel pamphlets with enticing photographs can stir up their interest. Or you can plan evenings focused on each country to be visited. Such parties can include distinctive food, local costumes, typical pictures, or decorations on the table and walls, and perhaps a unique product—smørbrod for Denmark, wooden shoes for Holland, brass rubbings for England. This kind of evening also provides a delightful aftermath of the trip; you can show slides or movies, wear clothing acquired abroad, use souvenir items as decorations, and perhaps have some conversation in the mother tongue of the country.

Planning Your Route

If you choose to follow a route that has already been planned (see Part Three), you will know approximately where you will be on each day of your trip. If you want to work in a visit to see friends, enjoy a festival on a holiday, or visit Parliament when it is open, you will need to list these special interests and plan around them. We sketch out our specific priorities on a sheet of paper and then fill in the days between (with a supply of erasers handy as we study maps and guides to estimate just how long it might take to drive). We look at the directness of the proposed route, the kind of roads available, and terrain that might cause us undue delay; we think of possible side excursions, and allow for days of relaxation. We erase and delete as choices are made and remade until we end up with (we hope) a manageable trip; then we neatly copy it onto an index card or two. On the card we list starting and stopping locations for each day, with the approximate mileage and estimated driving time. Useful planning maps can be obtained from AAA, Rand McNally, or map stores that carry European maps.

SAMPLE ROUTE AND MILEAGE CHART: TWO ALTERNATIVE PLANS FOR A 22-DAY TRIP FROM ENGLAND TO ITALY AND BAVARIA

Date		Plan 1 Place	Mileage	Plan 2 Place	Mileage
From Cambridge to:					
April	3	Cologne	377	Cologne	377
	4	Basel	308	Lucerne	366
	5	Como	225	Venice	343
	6	Como/Milan	—	Venice	—
	7	Como	—	Florence	167
	8	Sorrento	550	Sorrento	288
	9	Sorrento/Vesuvius	—	Sorrento/Vesuvius	—
	10	Sorrento/Capri	—	Sorrento/Capri	—

Date		Plan 1		Plan 2	
		Place	Mileage	Place	Mileage
April	11	Amalfi/Pioppi	80	Amalfi/Pioppi	80
	12	Pioppi	—	Pioppi	—
	13	Pioppi	—	Pioppi	—
	14	Pioppi	—	Pioppi	—
	15	Florence	370	Rome	236
	16	Florence	—	Como	365
	17	Venice	167	Como/Milan	—
	18	Venice	—	Como	—
	19	Grossweil	185	Grossweil	278
	20	Grossweil/Innsbruck	—	Innsbruck	—
	21	Garmisch	—	Garmisch	—
	22	Grossweil	—	Grossweil	—
	23	Brussels	542	Cologne	405
	24	Cambridge	263	Cambridge	377
Total mileage:			3,067		3,282
		9 campsites, 12 layover days, 10 driving days		10 campsites, 11 layover days, 11 driving days	

We chose to follow Plan 1 knowing very well that we had planned to cover more distance than seemed quite reasonable in twenty-two days. We wanted to visit relatives in Pioppi (in Southern Italy) and friends in Grossweil (in Bavaria) and therefore were fully aware of the reasons for our overplanning. We knew that if we did not want to give up any of our major stops we might have to drive long hours. Most of our choices were favorite locations from previous trips which we yearned to visit again. We went into the trip knowing that we might have to push a bit and enjoyed it in spite of a few stressful situations—detours, wet weather, arriving too late at campsites and pitching tents in the dark. All people camping through Europe have to decide how much they will put up with to do what they want to do.

Estimating Your Expenses and Getting Money

Once the route has been planned you can work up a cost estimate. We list all categories of expense such as campsite fees, gasoline costs (based on the total mileage and the cost per litre in each country), highway tolls, ferries, tickets, entrance fees to museums or other entertainment, food costs (estimated on the cost per day in each country multiplied by the number of days there), meals out, launderettes, sports equipment rental, postcards, gifts, and a slush fund for miscellaneous expenses. Of course, no matter how careful you are there is no guarantee that your costs will actually match your estimates. After taking several trips during the same year, we learned to be wary of certain types of expenses that tended to skyrocket—eating out, snacks, ferry costs in high season, sightseeing in cities—and felt confident about those that tended to remain stable. In any case, you will feel more comfortable with a ballpark figure as you order traveler's checks and plan to make an emergency fund somehow available.

Getting money in a hurry in Europe is not easy. Years ago, as impecunious Fulbright scholars (or "halfbrights," because we were trying to support two people on the stipend of $156 a month), we started on a trip with the assurance that a check from the USA would be sent on when it arrived in our local bank in England. What we did not know was that the check had in fact arrived on schedule, but was sitting in another branch of the same bank in London. We spent many fruitless hours during the trip trying to obtain our own money and only succeeded when a kindly American Express clerk in Norway waived the rules and allowed us to charge cash to our account. Even with a bank account in one branch of an American bank in London, we found that it took three weeks to cash a check in another branch of the same bank; therefore we made advance arrangements to cash checks without waiting.

In our years abroad we have learned more about beating the banking system in Europe—how to cope with problems that never occur to most Americans, who are offered more credit than they need through junk mail. Before the last trip we made all sorts of advance arrangements and did achieve a smoothly running banking relationship with a British bank. We also armed ourselves with both British and American credit cards and knew where each might be acceptable. Even simple problems can be difficult. Banking hours vary a great deal and are likely to be sparse during holidays. In every case, it pays to think through your financial needs and plan how you are going to get the money in advance.

SAMPLE COST ESTIMATE: 24-DAY TRIP FROM ENGLAND TO ITALY AND BAVARIA (1977 PRICES)

Item	Estimated	Spent
Gasoline for 3,000 miles	$346	$290
Ferry	176	176
Campsite fees for 13 nights	65	78
Meals out	100	98
Entrance Fees, postcards, cog railway, vaporetto	74	106
Tolls	50	33
Gifts	33	33
Miscellaneous (showers, Gaz refills, phone)	25	20
Camping insurance	9	9
Total cost	$878	$843

We did not count food either in our estimate or our total expenses because we would have spent the same amount living at home. In fact, we brought canned goods from England for a thirteen-day trip and supplemented that stock as we traveled and needed to buy perishable foods—which cost us $80 en route. We expected high gasoline costs based on estimated total mileage and average price per litre because we did not really know the exact cost at the pumps we would use in each country. We did know the ferry cost and booked ahead for that. Campsite fees varied widely, so we picked $5 a night as a reasonable average; in fact, we found many that were much lower because some campgrounds were barely open in April and were not charging full rates. The highest fees were in Sorrento (almost $10); the lowest were in Como ($2.50). We chose to have more meals out on this trip than we usually do. Many of them were noontime dinners in Venice, Milan, Capri, or Florence when we had left the car in a parking lot and were enjoying the area on foot. Entrance fees, postcards for the children's albums, the vaporetto (transportation by boat on the canals of Venice), and the cog railway up to the top of the Zugspitze were very difficult to estimate. Our miscellaneous category included much smaller expenses; the gifts we bought for our hosts before we left were known expenses. Again, tolls are difficult to estimate in advance for a trip you have not taken.

Purchasing Insurance

We purchased insurance for our camping gear and clothing for this trip because we had heard the usual tales about the prevalence of thievery in Italy. Young men on motor scooters are notorious for snatching purses and disappearing in a flash. The campground we chose outside Venice was barely open, with just a few campers around. We felt reasonably safe there until the next morning at 7 A.M. when a crew of workers appeared at the hotel next to the campground. We had thought it was not open and had purposely pitched our tents in the corner right next to it, away from other campers, for privacy as well as a superb view of the sea. There was nothing we could do except take the ferry into Venice, leaving our camping equipment zipped in the tents (which of course one can't lock) and try to keep our minds on other things all day. When we drove in that night, we were all on the edges of our seats, straining to see if our tents were in fact still there, then hurriedly unzipping each tent to see if it had been cleaned out—fortunately, nothing had been touched. Camping insurance is easy to purchase through automobile clubs and camping organizations in Europe (for example, AA, RAC, or Caravan Club in England) and is probably worth the small cost to save you worry about an unlikely (though possible) heist of your gear.

Passports and Customs

Before you leave for your European camping trip, you will need to allow enough time to get passports, which are available from any federal or state court authorized by law to naturalize aliens or at passport agencies of the U.S. Department of State in large cities. Each application requires two passport photos (2½ x 2½ to 3 x 3 inches), proof of citizenship such as a birth certificate or expired passport, and identification, which may be your driver's license or expired passport. There is a fee for each passport—$14 at this time. Your passport is good for five years. Visas are not necessary for most European countries. A recent smallpox vaccination certificate (within three years) is advisable for your return to the United States.

For information on current customs regulations, write for *Customs Hints for Returning U.S. Residents*, available from the U.S. Government Printing Office, Washington, D.C. 20402. It's a good idea to bring sales slips along for previously purchased European cameras, clothing, watches, and jewelry to avoid paying duty again.

GETTING THERE

Choosing Your Airfare

Travel by charter flight has been a booming industry, and the recent fare war among transatlantic airlines has made Europe more accessible than California from the East Coast. *Real* competition between the airlines has finally turned air travel into a buyer's market, with more choice in fares and booking conditions than ever before. But you must work harder to sort out the various possibilities and combinations or find a really sharp travel agent who will do the work and explain all the possibilities to you: charters, prepaid fares, special excursion fares, standing in line on a first-come, first-served basis, paying a premium (often small) for a reservation rather than waiting in long airport lines. Fares differ significantly during the low, shoulder, and peak seasons; shifting your vacation by a week or two may be worth it. You can write for a current copy of *Consumer's Guide to Air Charters* from the Civil Aeronautics Board, 1825 Connecticut Avenue N.W., Washington, DC. 20428. Travel agents usually have information and booklets on the special prices and features of transatlantic carriers.

Transatlantic carriers with many scheduled flights to Western Europe are:

Air France
1350 Avenue of the Americas
New York, N.Y. 10019

Alitalia Airlines
1652 Statler Hilton Building
Buffalo, N.Y. 14202

BOAC
530 Fifth Ave.
New York, N.Y. 10017

Icelandic Airlines, Inc.
630 Fifth Ave.
New York, N.Y. 10020

KLM Royal Dutch Airlines
609 Fifth Ave.
New York, N.Y. 10017

Laker Travel Center
95-25 Queens Blvd.
Rego Park, N.Y.

Lufthansa German Airlines
680 Fifth Ave.
New York, N.Y. 10022

Pan American World Airways
Pan American Building
100 E. 42nd St.
New York, N.Y. 10017

Scandinavian Airlines System
138-02 Queens Blvd.
Jamaica, N.Y. 11435

Swissair
Bldg. 15, Kennedy International Airport
Jamaica, N.Y. 11430

TWA
605 Third Ave.
New York, N.Y. 10016

If possible, try to fly east at night and west during the day. This pattern will minimize your body's reaction to the five- or six-hour time change by giving you a short day before sleep when you lose time and a long day followed by a full night when you gain time. Allow one day after arrival to rest and adjust. Plan not to arrive on a holiday or the day before a holiday; when you feel rested and ready to buy provisions for your trip you will want the shops to be open.

Finding a Ship

The good old days of an inexpensive, relaxing sea voyage may be a thing of the past, but it is still possible to find reliable lines operating. Sailing dates are not as frequent as they once were.

Among the lines still offering travel by ship are:

Cunard (*Queen Elizabeth II*)
555 Fifth Ave.
New York, N.Y. 10017

Italian Line (*Leonardo da
    Vinci*)
1 Whitehall
New York, N.Y. 10004

March Shipping Passenger
    Services (*Lermontov*)
One World Trade Center
Suite 5257
New York, N.Y. 10048

Norwegian America Line
    (*Vistafjord* and *Sagafjord*)
29 Broadway
New York, N.Y. 10006

Polish Ocean Lines
    (*Stefan Batory*)
410 St. Nicolas Street
Montreal, Quebec H2Y 2P5

Some people prefer a combination of air and sea travel to
enjoy the simple pleasure of leisurely voyaging without consuming
too large a proportion of total vacation time. If you will be staying
abroad for an extended period of time, there may be an additional
advantage in such an arrangement, since it would otherwise be
necessary to ship some household goods either by rather slow sea
or quite costly air freight. Transatlantic airlines have shifted from
weight restrictions to size limitations on baggage, which totally
changes the way packing is done for a camping family. You can

actually ship more gear now if you package it carefully. At the end of our last trip, we were, as usual, sweating it out trying to cram too much gear into the right number of suitcases and duffel bags, when we decided to lay out our large plastic car-top cover, squash and pile a duffel, four folding chairs, one small table, and another duffel on top, and tie it tightly. After a struggle to force the unwieldy bundle into an illusion of smallness we were delighted when it passed by the clerk at the airline counter without question. The early stages of planning should be a series of questions which help you establish the full costs for alternative modes of getting there, with gear.

COLLECTING

When all these segments of a total plan are reasonably firm, it is time to develop a packing list. Everyone seems to take too much the first time and trims the list more ruthlessly on each successive trip. If there is any question about needing an item on your list, leave it home. Fewer possessions are easier on the arms that carry them, the tempers of those who fit them into an intricate jigsaw puzzle in limited car space, and the patience of those who want to find things quickly in an orderly duffel bag. After a few days of struggling with too much stuff, most of us end up wearing the same thing over and over, wishing that the rest had been left at home. Like Thoreau's man of property weighed down by all his possessions, we begin to curse ourselves for bringing them in the first place.

Clothing

Before each trip we have collected booklets and packing lists from many airlines, luggage companies, and travel agents. Then, with a list of the clothing we have used on previous trips in hand, we check through new lists and add whatever makes sense for us. We always read travel columns in newspapers and magazines, watching for the occasional new idea that may turn out to be tremendously useful. Then we go into reverse with our old lists, culling out any items that were infrequently used to reduce the weight, clutter, and annoyance of too much baggage. Finally, we type out and make copies of a list of basic clothing for the entire family and hand each person one to adjust to his or her own needs and check off as items are packed. Assuming that launderettes will be available periodically, and that a little hand wash will be done occasionally, we have been able to travel happily for one or two months in the summer with the following for each person:

2 pairs long pants
5 shirts or tops
7 sets underwear
7 pairs socks
2 pairs heavy socks
1 pajamas or gown
1 robe or beachrobe
2 sweaters
1 light jacket
1 rain jacket
1 sweatshirt
1 bathing suit
2 pairs shorts
1 pair hiking boots
1 pair walking shoes
1 pair sandals
1 sun hat
1 hand towel
1 washcloth
2 bath towels
1 plastic laundry bag
1 dressy outfit

1 pair sunglasses
1 flashlight
1 sleeping bag
1 air mattress
1 cosmetic bag (soap in box, toothbrush, paste, deodorant, hand cream, comb, brush, shower cap, pills, other medical needs)

You may also want to take:

camera and film
deck of cards
journal and pens
needlepoint or other handwork
paperbacks
suntan cream
tissues
sewing kit
travel books
first aid kit
toilet paper
prescriptions for glasses

For a trip involving more city touring or visits with friends, additional dressier clothing could be added, such as a wrap skirt, long skirt, blazer, raincoat, scarves and accessories for a woman, or sport coat, slacks, ties, and raincoat for a man.

For a trip during spring or fall, possibly in rainy weather, you should add heavy pajamas, another sweater, a nylon windshirt, rain pants, a warm jacket, boots, warm gloves, a wool cap, a track suit, turtleneck tops, and ski underwear.

For a trip in cold weather you should add a ski jacket, scarf, ski gloves, winter boots, and other warm gear of your preference, as well as a low-temperature down sleeping bag of superior quality.

The goal is to take only what will actually be worn or used. Otherwise you will return resenting the gear that took up space without paying its way. Coordinate colors so that no item requires a specific match with another to cut down on duplication. And whenever you can, use nonwrinkle fabrics—a true boon to camping travelers who are forced to live from duffel bags and still look presentable.

Packing

The best advice is to take only what you can carry comfortably for a couple of blocks. One large soft piece of luggage, preferably a duffel bag that can change its shape to fit a tightly packed car, one soft carry-on bag that will fit easily under the seat ahead on a plane, and, for women, a large squashy purse should be ample. In addition, an empty duffel to use along the way for purchases and gifts is handy. You will need the other piece of luggage allowed by airlines to pack sleeping bags, cooking utensils, and other camping gear. We found additional lightweight duffel bags and a supply of rope or heavy twine very useful as we struggled to combine it all into the allowable number of pieces.

Each piece of luggage should have an identification card on the outside as well as on the inside. We also made a design with tape on all pieces; this helped to identify them as they tumbled into the baggage claim area. Luggage locks and keys help to keep the contents intact, and a complete list of the entire contents of each piece is immediately useful if one gets lost.

When packing, we place all shoes in separate plastic bags, underwear in one bag, other small items in bags, tucking in several more for future use. Plastic bags make it easier to slip things in and out of a duffel bag and help you find what you want more quickly; otherwise everything sifts toward the bottom and the whole bag gets mussed after two or three searches. A duffel bag with a long zipper across the top can be packed in thirds, with clothing used less frequently on each end. An upright duffel bag may get disorderly unless you pack a number of items in a large plastic bag on top; this can then be lifted out intact to get at the second layer.

Children will find a small backpack very useful as a carry-on bag and can use it later as a car bag and for hikes. Toys, paperbacks, an extra sweater or jacket, slippers, cards or games, journal, pen, extra film, handwork such as needlepoint or a leather project can be slipped in. You may want to carry camera gear and film in a special bag, but make sure that it does not go through the X-ray machine at airports. A large purse is a convenient carrier for important documents such as passports and traveler's checks, tickets, and your itinerary. You can even make a liner with several zippers for greater security and ease in finding things.

Camping Equipment

For a short trip you will be happier with the absolute minimum of equipment. Oddly enough, it seems to be true that the same equipment will also do for a longer trip. Through a process of trial and error, you can discover which items mean a lot to you while traveling under canvas and which are not used much, if at all. About one-half of the following items will probably be essential for you:

air mattresses or foam pads
asbestos mitts
breadboard
broom, small
can opener
chairs, folding
clothesline and pins
cook kit
corkscrew
corn tongs (for turning bacon)
dishcloth or sponge
dishpans

dishtowels

dishwashing liquid or soap bar

funnel

ground sheet

juice container

kettle

knives

lanterns and flashlights

mallet

matches

packsack for camping gear

paper towels

plastic bags

plates, cups, bowls

pump for air mattresses

rope

salt and pepper

scissors

scouring pads

shopping bag

silverware

sleeping bags (for appropriate temperature range)

string

stove

table, small

tablecloth, plastic

tent

tent stakes

tools (long-handled spoon, slotted spoon, pancake turner, soup ladle)

tools (hammer, pliers, wrenches, screwdrivers, knife, grommet kit, sewing kit)

trash bags

water jug
wax paper
wind shield for stove

Travelers who do not own camping equipment may prefer to rent it upon arrival in Europe. Many large camping stores in major cities offer this service. We chose to bring sleeping bags and air mattresses with us and bought the rest in England. Because camping has been very popular there for a long time, Europe offers even more camping equipment than America does, and we enjoy shopping for just the right gear. We were delighted to increase our collection of tents with a French tent that was light, easy to erect, dry, and very comfortable. We bought additional small two-person tents for each child to give them a little respite from togetherness. These tents weighed almost nothing and were dry and easy to manage; they also increased our capability for backpacking and mountain hiking. For those with very small children or those who prefer camping with more comforts and accessories, renting a small camping vehicle or tent trailer may be preferable. Or, if you want comfort all the way, you can rent and tow a caravan. On an earlier trip when our children were 3 and 6 years old, we bought a camper, which solved the tent problem except for one tent we had brought along to let the family spread out.

It is important to select just the right stove for your culinary pleasure. We have finally settled on two small, easily stored Gaz stoves which provide us with quick heat for a two-pot meal. Gaz butane refills are easily available anywhere in Europe. In the past we have used Optimus, Primus, and Svea, burning gas, white gas, and alcohol, respectively. Although all performed well, none was as convenient or fast as the small butane stove. Heavy, complicated two-burner liquid fuel stoves are usually not worth the space they take unless you are traveling with a camper ot tent trailer.

The other assorted equipment you need is easily available in any camping store. We bought three large plastic boxes and a number of smaller ones to hold our dishes, utensils, and other gear.

They stacked in one packsack, keeping everything orderly. When we made camp we would lay out the plastic boxes in the same order in the bell end of the tent extension. The entire family knew where every item could be found, no matter where we were. The other packsack held the two small plastic dishpans, then the cook kit with the kettle on top. All the other cooking necessaries fit around these items so the cook could unpack gear always knowing where things were, while others erected tents.

European campers carry lanterns which we felt were too bulky to take home with us. Instead we bought a fluorescent light that hooked up to our car battery, and found that very bright, compact, and handy (it also doubled as an emergency vehicle light). In addition we had flashlights for each person and a battery-powered lantern for each tent.

Most European campgrounds do not furnish tables as American campgrounds do, so one must bring something to sit on. We could have gotten along very well with air mattresses to lounge on but did find little folding canvas sand chairs much easier on our backs (though they were hard to get up from). We also bought a small low folding table which came in very handy while we were cooking. It held a candle in a can at dusk, and later provided a flat surface for card games.

Camp housekeeping was not difficult once we had persuaded everyone to take off shoes before going into tents. During rainy weather we placed our Wellington boots (English rubber boots) carefully between the tent and the fly sheet with a plastic bag over the top to keep them dry. We had a ground sheet covering the area in front of the tent, and a little whiskbroom swept away any bits of dirt that otherwise would have been tracked into sleeping quarters. A camper's entire attitude and pleasure during a spell of bad weather can depend on having at least one clean, dry place to retreat to.

Many European tents are now sold with an "extension" which adds a "living room" to your tent in bad weather. We camped without one for a while in October, but after nine days of rain decided we needed an extension. We sewed together two nylon fly sheets to make an extension that, though not completely water-proof along the ridge, was quite an improvement over the open air and rain. It had two long zippers on each side so that the side away from the wind could be opened up and held with poles. One end zipped right onto our larger tent; the opposite end was made in a bell shape and contained our "kitchen area" with boxes all lined up on a ground sheet. The center area was large enough for five small chairs, the folding table, and a happy family playing games at night—out of the wet!

For a short trip abroad it makes sense to buy all your equipment at home to avoid the frustrations and delays of shopping after arrival. However, if you prefer to rent or buy equipment when you arrive, the yellow pages are a good place to begin. Camping stores abound all over Europe, and many of them rent equipment. Most of them stock a complete selection of anything you will need. Having compared prices in various camping stores throughout central England, I found the differences in the cost of cooking equipment and camping accessories insignificant. Tents are another matter, ranging from high-quality light mountain tents to elaborate, large framed tents with many "rooms"—both expensive purchases—to cheaper less well-made discount versions. Buying a tent requires careful research in advance, but since many British, French, Italian, and Scandinavian tents are marketed in mountaineering and camping stores in America, you can set your requirements and do most of your homework before you go.

If you do decide to buy your equipment at one of the starting points for our suggested itineraries, *the following stores, among many others, have a full range of equipment:*

LONDON AND   Blacks of Greenock
VICINITY   53/4 Rathbone Pl.
                    London (also in Edinburgh)

                    Camping Centre
                    Kilburn Warehouse, Lonsdale Rd. N.W.6
                    London

Crystal Palace Camping
5/7 Church Rd.
Crystal Palace, London

Eton's Outdoor Centre
100-106 Haydons Rd.
Wimbledon

Lillywhite's
Piccadilly Circus
London

Millets Camp and Clothing Store
445 Oxford St.
London

Touchwood Sports, Ltd.
40 Cowley Rd.
Oxford

COPENHAGEN   Spejder Sport
Norre Farimagsgade 39
Copenhagen

AMSTERDAM   Neef Sport
Hartenstraat 7-9
Amsterdam

N.V. Sportmagazijn Perry Van Der Kar
Binnenhof 7
Amstelveen (suburb)
 also at 93-101 Kalverstraat
 and 149-157 Ceinturbaan, Amsterdam

Equipment for Children

If you are traveling with children, you will find that, depending upon their age, you can get by with very few of the toys and belongings that are considered essential at home. We have often taken too much. It is better to take just a few things and let the children have the fun of picking something out in one of the magnificent toy shops found in nearly every town and city throughout Europe. While camping, children are usually busy exploring the area, playing on swings and in sandboxes, swimming, playing ball, and communicating with other children (who probably speak another language—they usually get along beautifully without either language). A few miniature cars, a doll or two, some puzzles, coloring books, and a ball will do.

Tourist Information

In the early stages of planning a trip you may want to write to the national tourist office for each country you plan to visit. If you are taking children, put their names on your request for information, maps, brochures on festivals, sports features, castles, local crafts, zoos, and the like. This will give them the fun of receiving a deluge of mail. Reading done in anticipation of the adventures to come will enhance their enjoyment and learning during the trip.

New York addresses for some of the national tourist offices follow:

Austrian State Tourist
  Department
545 Fifth Ave.
New York, N.Y. 10017

Belgian Tourist Bureau
745 Fifth Ave.
New York, N.Y. 10022

British Travel Association
680 Fifth Ave.
New York, N.Y. 10019

Danish Travel Office
75 Rockefeller Plaza
New York, N.Y. 10019

Finnish National Travel
    Office
75 Rockefeller Plaza
New York, N.Y. 10019

French Government Tourist
    Offices
610 Fifth Ave.
New York, N.Y. 10020

German Tourist Information
    Office
630 Fifth Ave.
New York, N.Y. 10020

Irish Tourist Office
590 Fifth Ave.
New York, N.Y. 10036

Italian Government Tourist
    Office
630 Fifth Ave.
New York, N.Y. 10020

Luxembourg Consulate
    General
1 Dag Hammarskjold Plaza
New York, N.Y. 10017

Netherlands National Tourist
  Office
576 Fifth Ave.
New York, N.Y. 10036

Norwegian National Tourist
  Office
75 Rockefeller Plaza
New York, N.Y. 10019

Spanish Tourist Office
589 Fifth Ave.
New York, N.Y. 10017

Swedish National Travel
75 Rockefeller Plaza
New York, N.Y. 10019

Swiss National Tourist Office
608 Fifth Ave.
New York, N.Y. 10020

We took along a stack of photos of our life at home to show friends in Europe. Some children may enjoy putting together a book showing special features of their area, school, friends, and general information about the United States. People we have met are always interested in what it is *really* like in the States. If you particularly want to meet people during your travels there are programs such as "Meet the Danes" available. Local tourist offices in each town often have information about such opportunities.

Children may want to give their friends a copy of addresses where mail can be received during the trip. It is always fun for them to get mail from home. You can pick up mail in American Express offices, Thomas Cook & Sons, or Poste Restante (general delivery).

COUNTDOWN FOR CAMPERS

In order to aid your planning, we have organized a countdown list by months before departure. The deadlines are not precise for every trip, but they can help you to prevent missing something you want to do and to avoid unneeded flurry and raw nerves during the last weeks before departure.

Six months before departure (or when you know you are going)

Write to national tourist offices for information and maps.

Write to airlines and shipping companies for schedules and fares.

Write to car rental and purchase companies, both in the United States and abroad.

Begin clipping and collecting articles and information on the places you want to visit.

Organize all the incoming material by category or country.

Keep information obtained by phone in a folder or notebook.

Check your library for books on the countries and regions you plan to visit.

Brush up on your previous foreign language skills.

Plan an itinerary within Europe.

Four months before departure

Make reservations by air or sea (earlier during peak summer periods of transatlantic travel).

Make the arrangements for car purchase, including shipment home.

Apply for passports.

Make appointments for shots.

Make ferry reservations within Europe if you will be traveling during holiday periods.

Make arrangements for rental of your home (if you will be away long enough to make this feasible and desirable).

Two months before departure

Obtain camping carnet.*

---

*A document of identification. It may be left in the camp office instead of a passport (until your bill is paid), and it sometimes entitles you to discounts on campground fees.

Collect health records from doctors.

Make arrangements for house utilities and other services during absence.

Purchase needed clothing and equipment.

Make reservations for car rental (both in United States and abroad).

One month before departure

Buy traveler's checks.

Get letter of credit from your bank.

Buy film.

Buy gifts for friends in Europe.

Prepare your itinerary with addresses for mail to be received in Europe.

Make final arrangements for home and pets in your absence.

One week before departure

Pack as much as possible.

Make arrangements for your mail at home.

Check to make sure you have all tickets and documents.

We have found that when some of these things-to-be-done slip down from week to week on the list, the final week can be horrendous. With all the last-minute excitement and fatigue we always wish we had begun earlier.

HOUSEHOLDING

Selecting a Base for Longer Stays

For those who are lucky enough to spend six months or a year abroad, finding a home in a village or an apartment in a city can be an unnerving experience. But there are effective ways to make a good start before leaving home. Some academic communities offer help through organizations like the Society for Visiting Scholars in Cambridge or the Newcomers in Oxford. Sometimes it is possible to live in university or college housing temporarily while you are house-hunting. Advance inquiries will result in an exchange of letters with such societies and with realtors (called estate agents in England) to help locate specific houses. You can also answer ads in foreign newspapers, in the *International Herald Tribune*, in the newsletters of agencies promoting foreign exchanges, or in the catalogues of house-swapping networks. Some college alumni magazines include listings of flats and homes available for rent abroad, and friends or acquaintances can suggest realtors to contact in a specific area.

Some people hesitate to take a place sight unseen and prefer to make a concentrated search after arrival. Others, especially those with young families, prefer the convenience of a smooth entry to life abroad. Finding a temporary flat for a week or two in advance is a middle way. You will have to be honest about your own (and your children's, if you are taking them) anxiety levels and adaptibility when making this choice.

There are a number of home-exchange organizations in existence. They can help you rent your home while you are gone and locate the home of someone abroad during the same period. In some cases a direct swap is arranged which can even include cars and pets. When such arrangements work smoothly, they save a great deal of time and effort, and they can solve problems (for example, the long quarantine for pets) that are otherwise difficult. *A partial list of home-exchange brokers includes:*

Inquiline
Box 208
Katonah, N.Y. 10536

Professional Courtesy, Inc.
601 Beachview Dr.
St. Simons Island, Ga. 31522

The Vacation Exchange Club
350 Broadway
New York, N.Y. 10013

Home Vacation Exchange
P.O. Box 278
Winnetka, Ill. 60093

Interchange
56 W. 45th St.
New York, N.Y. 10036

There is a fair amount of extra planning to be done when you
will be away for an extended period of time. Our last adventure in
Europe lasted for a year, with twelve weeks of travel under canvas
during that time. We chose to rent a home by mail, which allowed
us to have things sent ahead. Also, we then had an address to use
for arranging various business affairs such as insurance, banking,
and professional correspondence.

We began making lists of things to do here and things to do
over there and organized them by weeks, both to avoid slipping up
on something important and to get some sense of progress in ac-
complishing the necessary miscellaneous chores. Checking off
many items in one week was a cause for celebration. Four weeks
before we left our list included: update house inventory and take to
safety deposit box; compile income tax information necessary for
computing and filing from overseas; arrange to pay all insurance
premiums once for the year; collect health records from the doctor
and have necessary shots; call in address changes for utilities,
banks, and other services; get international driver's license from
AAA; type Christmas card list; and call car rental agencies to
reserve cars in New York, Luxembourg, and Dover. Three weeks
before departure the list looked like this: get student identity cards
for the children; send change-of-address cards to friends and relatives; mark all luggage with name tags and a special design in tape;
buy film; set up banking arrangements in Europe by letters from
banks and employers here. Two weeks before departure: settle
final arrangements for purchase of a car to be picked up in London
on the second day after arrival in Luxembourg; find a recent currency converter; order dog tags with the name of friends who will

keep the dogs; have extra house keys made for renters; diagram garden so renters will know where not to spade; make a list of appliance repair numbers and household information for renters; clear drawers and closets. The last week is always hectic and by then it is too late for lists—you simply hope you haven't forgotten anything.

After farewell parties, cleaning the house, and inevitable last-minute details to attend to, we always look forward to the moment of relief that comes as we settle down into our airline seats. It is nice to relax, sleep a lot, and enjoy the feeling of being in between two parts of your life.

You will want to settle into your new home for a week or two before planning the focus of your first trip. We have always had thoughtful neighbors who have helped us learn the ropes of shopping, early closing hours, utilities, and other routines in the village or area. As you meet people you will hear about the holiday they took recently or where they would like to go and you will find yourself becoming interested in planning your first trip.

Choosing and Timing Your Trips

During your stay abroad, if you have children of school age with you, you will want to travel when they are on holiday. Fortunately, English schools (and many on the continent) provide a number of holidays during the year, although they continue longer into the summer. They are also understanding when parents add a few days onto a trip that may be as educational as being in school. Fall and spring are ideal seasons for camping; summer is crowded but certainly possible. When you have a home base you can plan trips of any length, from a long weekend to several weeks. You are able to plan and provision before the trip starts and return again to a familiar environment. You can change and add to your equipment from trip to trip. It helps to keep all your camping gear in one place, such as in a camping closet, so items can just be checked off as they are packed into the car. You will find that you can estimate the length of time you really enjoy camping and not extend trips too long. You may well appreciate periods of home life in a familiar routine after the stimulation of travel.

FINDING THE RIGHT TRANSPORTATION

Choosing your mode of transportation for a camping trip is reasonably complicated because it depends upon the answer to a number of preliminary questions. How many are there in your party? How much space do you and your traveling companions need while driving? Will you want to sleep in a vehicle, in tents, or in a combination of both? What is your minimum acceptable level of comfort? What sort of terrain will your trip cover? How long will it last? The right choice of vehicle will probably be a compromise of some sort, balancing comfort, space, cost, gasoline consumption, ease of handling, ruggedness, the convenience of pick-up and drop-off points, and possible future use of the vehicle either abroad or back home. In any case, you will want to consider the advantages and disadvantages of four possible ways of acquiring a vehicle: rental, leasing, purchasing and reselling, and purchasing to ship home.

Automobile Rental, Lease, or Purchase

Renting a car often can be the most economical way to travel as well as the most convenient. The breakeven point between public and private transportation is usually reached when you have more than one or two persons traveling together; and for camping ventures the convenience of having your own vehicle is almost always worth the extra money because it frees you from timetables and gives you access to places not easily reached in any other way.

Rental cars are available in all major European cities. *Information on cars, caravans, or campmobiles can be obtained from:*

> Car Plan Headquarters
> 420 Lexington Ave.
> New York, N.Y. 10017
>
> Continental Campers, Inc.
> 1194 Walnut St.
> P.O. Box 306
> Newton, Mass. 02161
>
> Eurocamper Tourmobiles,
>   Inc.
> 170 Broadway
> New York, N.Y. 10038
>
> Europe by Car, Inc.
> 45 Rockefeller Plaza
> New York, N.Y. 10020
>
> Kemwel Group, Inc.
> 247 W. 12th St.
> New York, N.Y. 10014
>
> Nemet Auto International
> 153-03 Hillside Avenue
> Jamaica, N.Y. 11432

Avis, Hertz, and other American rental agents can also make these arrangements. Be aware of the fact that rates differ from country to country. Sometimes you can do better by waiting until you arrive to strike a bargain. In high season, this may not be worth the risk.

We have chosen to purchase a car in Europe, timing the sale of our cars here carefully. At one point, a camper was perfect for our family of young children, with a tent as a supplement. Later we found that a small station wagon was adequate for our camping needs. The purchase and documentation, including insurance, can be arranged in advance by a dealer at home so that the car is waiting upon your arrival in Europe. It is possible that local dealers do not have the expertise to handle delivery abroad, so you may want to choose a company that specializes in such delivery. An article in the *New York Times* described the buying of used vans or cars on the Strand in London. We have had no experience here; you can take your chances if you wish!

Leasing can also be arranged. For stays longer than one month, leasing is usually cheaper than renting because there is no mileage charge. It is also possible to buy a car with the understanding that it may be sold back, sometimes at a guaranteed price.

It can be useful to purchase an international driving permit from AAA before leaving home. Information on international road signs, mountain passes, and tunnels is also available. Gasoline coupons for Italy and some other countries can be purchased in advance. Make arrangements to buy gas coupons before you enter the country because they will save you a great deal in a country where gas prices are very high. In some areas you can buy them just before you cross the border, but the office may be closed when you need them.

Caravan Rental

Rental caravans are very popular and easily available in England through International Caravan Holidays, 292 Lower High St., Watford, Hertfordshire, England. You can reach other agencies by contacting the AAA in America, the Automobile Association or Royal Automobile Club in England, or the yellow pages for the city in which you will begin your tour. The national automobile clubs in each country can make arrangements or send you the name and address of the appropriate agency. The British Tourist Authority publishes a book *(Camping and Caravan Sites)* which has a list of caravan rental companies.

Car Shipment Home

Some companies still include free car shipment home in the cost of the car. Otherwise, there are a number of agencies available. North Sea ports (Antwerp, Rotterdam, Bremen, and Hamburg) provide more sailings and cheaper prices than most other ports. E. H. Harms and Company, Hansestrasse 5, Bremen, Germany has offices in a number of ports. AAA, or other automobile clubs, can also make arrangements for you.

Ferry Transportation

There are wild variations in the costs of ferries depending upon the time of year. The prices during high season are much higher than during low season, and the rates also skyrocket on certain days just before and just after holidays during the rest of the year. At times it is imperative to book ahead to avoid long lines and the frustration of missing one sailing after another. Europeans travel a great deal on holidays and they have learned to plan ahead. There are a number of possible ferries between the Continent and Britain, varying in length of sailing time, cost, and convenience. It takes a bit of studying to figure out the best possible route to fit in with your total itinerary. You may want to book ahead through a firm such as Car Ferry Enquiries, Ltd., 9a Spur Rd., Isleworth, Middlesex, England, TW75BD.

You can obtain information on ferries from automobile clubs, travel agents, or by purchasing a pamphlet (available in bookstores in England or by mail) such as *Car Ferries 19-*, published by Car Ferry Enquiries, Ltd. This booklet includes information on Cross Channel, Mediterranean, North Sea, Scandinavian, and Irish ferries. Rates are listed by size of car as well as by day of the year.

3

coping

FINDING GOOD CAMPSITES

Once the planning and packing have been done and you are on the way, the physical conditions of travel can be crucial to the pleasures of the whole venture. You must consider your own and your traveling companions' tolerance of discomfort and provide easy ways of adapting to moods, weather, and plans that go awry. Traveling by automobile is convenient and flexible, with no timetables to meet, but it also can be intolerably confining if you drive too long. Experienced campers try to stop early enough each day to find an attractive campsite before the best ones are taken. They also want to have time left over for a relaxing swim or walk before dinner. Such a daily pattern allows time for eating, washing dishes in the light, and for relaxation. If there are children with you, they will have a chance to play games and get acquainted with their peers, often one of the most rewarding experiences of the whole trip for them.

Those who have not camped before may be appalled by the prospect of uncertainty or discomfort, thinking that such travel is only for young students trying to find themselves by hitchhiking around. And those who roll into a city campground at 10:00 P.M. in August may well be put off by a crowded site, noise, and the prospect of setting up camp hurriedly—perhaps with tired children. But many European families camp whenever they travel, and when you meet them you will notice that they are generally well equipped, well organized, and comfortable. Ordinarily you can set and meet personal priorities all over Europe in the form of hot showers, lovely views, attractive sites, and quiet neighbors. As you travel, these priorities will shift, depending upon the weather, the number of days planned in each area, the activities and sights nearby, and individual preferences. Some people insist on beautiful campsites for longer stays but will settle for something less desirable for one-night stands in between; others would rather travel shorter distances and score every time. With a little experience and some honesty about what you want to do (not what you "should" do to "cover" the country), you will develop your own style and pace.

It is not easy to stick to a reasonable itinerary once you start investigating all the fascinating possibilities to be explored in any area. Some areas abound with castles, stately homes, zoos, cathedrals, museums, and minature villages, as well as special festivals. The problem becomes one of making choices about how long you want to stay, where you want to go next, and when you must leave to reach another destination. But the essential factor in all these choices is your ability to establish a series of enjoyable, if temporary, home bases. You need to be able to find good campsites quickly and easily.

Location

Unless you have traveled the same route before, you should allow time to search for a campsite that is pleasant and has the amenities you would like. A description in a campsite guide will give you basic information about amenities, but the view may be different as seen from another pair of eyes. We have found that for a one-night stand we are comfortable rolling in anytime before dusk (often very late during Northern European summers) and picking a site without too much looking around. It is nice to have cleanliness and lack of noise from close neighbors, but we have survived cheerfully when conditions were dreadful, knowing that we would be somewhere else the next night.

We quickly learned which campsite guides were accurate (See page 44) and which we could not count on at all. At lunch or while driving, we would read the descriptions and pick out one or more campsites to investigate in the area we were aiming for. For a long stay we were quite fussy about the view, locale, and reasonable facilities. In some beautiful areas it was not difficult to find the perfect spot. In or near cities we found crowded conditions and often ended up altering our plans to head for more beautiful sites in the suburbs or the surrounding countryside.

Desirable Amenities

On the whole, campgrounds on the Continent tend to be well planned, with trees separating sites, spotlessly clean bathroom and shower facilities, generally pleasant surroundings, washing machines, swimming pools and a well-stocked shop. In Britain we found many well-equipped campsites and a few quite primitive ones which were less costly and sometimes well worth it for an appealing lake or mountain view. The more primitive British campsites are generally old farms; often the bathrooms are built into barns and the sites themselves are on grass or meadow, complete with cows or sheep. In Scandinavia some of the campsites include little houses for cooking, washing dishes, and social gatherings.

Seasons and Holidays

As with every other aspect of travel during a particularly busy holiday weekend, finding a campsite can be difficult. If possible, it is wise to book in advance. Otherwise plan to arrive in time to find a site before they are all gobbled up. We tried to stop by 3:00 or 4:00 P.M. when we thought it might be difficult to find a spot. In Central Europe much of the summer is busy; we did not find this to be true in Scandinavia, except near ferries.

Most of our travel has been done off season (April through June, September, and October), which has some real advantages. We felt we could escape the tourist syndrome and all its attendant nonsense— higher prices, less interest on the part of people in places visited, more arrangements to make competing with other tourists. We did not encounter lines and waits at ferries, museums, restaurants, or castles. Sometimes we opened up campgrounds, and although we froze on some April nights when the temperature plummeted, it was worth it. Not being patient with crowds and lines, we prefer this leisurely and unharried kind of travel.

Campsite Guides

Most of the national tourist offices put out a guide listing all approved campsites in the country. Some of them include a star system indicating the quality of services provided. You can get these by writing in advance, sometimes as you go through customs, or in the local tourist offices as you travel.

Commercial guides list a variety of detail. Some of them list the kind of water available (ocean, lake, river); the nature of the beach (shingle, rock, sand); sun on the sites (shady or exposed); sports available on site or nearby; difficulty for caravans; ground (grassy, sandy, rocky); and one listed a column entitled "exceptional natural beauty." One guide also includes annotated comments sent in by travelers on specific campsites. *Recommended guides include:*

AA Guide to Camping and Caravanning on the Continent. Published by the Automobile Association, Farnum House, Basingstoke, Hampshire, England RG21 2EA. This guide did not have listings for areas we happened to need. The listings it does have include specific details on facilities and some prices.

Campsites in Europe. Published by Rand McNally and Company, P.O. Box 7600, Chicago, Illinois 60680, for Charles Letts and Company, Ltd. This guide consistently includes more specific detail than any other we have seen. Campground location is indicated on maps in the front of the book with numbers indicating where detailed information is found. This guide is 8½ × 11 inches, an awkward size to carry.

Caravan Club Foreign Touring Handbook. Published by The Caravan Club, Bowmaker House, 55 St. James Street, London, England SW1A 1LA. An excellent guide with annotated comments by travelers. Only includes campsites that are known by its staff and members; therefore some areas are more fully covered than others. Some prices and some directions are given for finding the campgrounds.

Europa Camping and Caravaning. Published by Reise and Ver-kehrsverlag, Postfach 800830, Stuttgart, Germany. This guide in-cludes a great deal of information about each campground. There are maps, information on ferries, currency exchange tables, and international price lists.

EATING

Part of the fun of travel is the opportunity to taste special foods in each country. As we drove through Scandinavia, the sight-ing of another berry stand brought great joy to children and par-ents alike. Cloud berries, like their name, were out of this world! In Denmark we tried smørbrod (open-faced sandwiches with a variety of special toppings) a number of times and could easily assemble the ingredients to make our own. Indonesian food is very good and popular in the Netherlands because many Dutch people lived there before World War II and learned to cook these foods expertly. Of course, in both the Netherlands and Switzerland, chocolate is superb, and Cadbury's provides a similar temptation in England. In Paris we have tried Alsatian cooking, with huge plat-ters of sauerkraut and sausage topped with champagne, as well as more typical French cuisine. Italy offers an unimaginable variety of pasta dishes as well as special treats like veal with Marsala. Sauerbraten in Germany, apple strudel in Austria, raclette and fondue in Switzerland are all remembered with pleasure. In Eng-land we picked blackberries along the hedges in the fall and made beautiful fresh desserts, as well as enjoyed roast beef and York-shire pudding, plowman's lunches, and rum trifle for dessert.

Some of the pleasure associated with these special foods comes from eating in an atmosphere that is certainly authentic. Some of these foods and many others can be brought to the campsite and enjoyed there, like fish and chips taken straight from the shop wrapped in newspaper and enjoyed while piping hot. In seaport towns crab can be purchased cracked and ready to be eaten with a supply of paper napkins. Fresh bread is available daily in most countries, perhaps still warm from the baker's oven in the early morning, and special pastries abound in most parts of Western Europe.

Campsite Cooking

Camping allows people to "cater for themselves," which saves bundles of money. You can lay in a stock of canned goods in countries that have cheaper prices and use them with extra pleasure in more expensive neighboring countries. Perishable foods can be purchased en route either from supermarkets or from little shops wherever you happen to be. We usually purchased basic supplies from a supermarket where the prices were on the products, allowing us to muse a little with a list in hand. When purchasing for a trip, we estimated the number of meals we thought we would eat in camp, subtracting those we might eat out or bring in from local stores. Usually we chose to eat out at lunch while sightseeing. It is often more convenient, and far less expensive, to prepare dinners in the cozy atmosphere of your own campsite with a candle stuck in a can for a glow and perhaps a cup of sherry or local wine to warm the heart. Our children enjoyed selecting favorite foods from our stock of canned goods and acting as chef for the night. After dinner we had plenty of time to go for a walk, enjoy the view or a sunset, just loll around, and meet other campers to look over their collections of ingenious and practical camping gear.

Local Wines and Beers

Wines never taste as good as they do right where they are produced. We did a lot of our own wine tasting and came upon some fine local wines that are not exported—a real incentive to return! Beers that command such a high price when imported into the United States are an affordable treat while in the country of origin. It is easy to become spoiled with Lowenbrau or Heinecken's available at a decent price. A special pleasure in Germany and England is sampling the draft beer. It is now possible to get a list of pubs serving totally natural beer ("real" beer) in many areas of England.

Cooking by Computer

Organizing a total food plan in advance certainly makes travel more enjoyable. "Cooking by computer" involves making up a set of index cards with a menu for one day, including recipes that are more involved than just opening cans, and a shopping list of ingredients. A separate card can list staples to keep on hand. When preparing for a trip just pull the cards for the menus you plan to use, add the staple card, and jot down the number of total items needed on your shopping list. Another card can list cooking utensils and equipment that need to be packed.

If that seems like a great deal of work, you can also "cook by chart." Make columns for breakfast, lunch, dinner, and snacks across the top and list the days of the trip down the sheet. Then fill in the menus by day and add up the number of items needed for your shopping list.

We carry a very small notebook with foods listed by category, and enter new recipes as we go. Over the years we have collected some interesting combinations. We are always on the lookout for new products that do not need refrigeration, as well as an expanding collection of dehydrated and freeze-dried foods.

Packing the mound of cans and boxes for a long trip is not easy, but at least they decrease as the trip progresses. We use up the largest cans early in the trip and end up with a few boxes and packets of lighter foods. Our car has a storage compartment underneath the deck where one layer of cans can lie in rows. The chef for the day simply raises the lid to see what we have and makes his or her choice for dinner. During the day we carry a separate lunchbox with items like a small cutting board, knife, plastic tablecloth, napkins, cups, jar of peanut butter, jelly, cheese, and meat spreads. Cartons can also be used to hold canned goods as long as the cans are in some kind of order so they all needn't be removed for a meal.

A sample list of nonperishable staples includes the following:

bouillon
cereal, hot
cocoa
coffee
crackers
fruit-drink mix
honey
jelly
marmalade
pancake mix
powdered milk
salad cream
salt and pepper
sugar
syrup
tea

Sample Menu Plans for One Week

In planning the menus below we have omitted some recipes that we have usually associated with camping in the United States. Most European campgrounds do not permit open fires, which does away with "s'mores" (graham cracker, roasted marshmallow, and chocolate sandwich) from our days of camping as children, freshly caught fish cooked on a grill in canoe country, and other foods that taste particularly good cooked over a fire. When using a two-burner Coleman stove in the past we have enjoyed foods that can be cooked slowly without much trouble. However, the stoves that most of us will probably choose to use in Europe will be small and the fuel will be too expensive for the luxury of slow cooking. There-fore we lean heavily on canned goods, dehydrated and freeze-dried packets, and other foods that do not take long to heat. Foods that some of us think rather unexciting right out of a can taste better after a day spent outside exploring a new area and storing up memories. The addition of herbs, grated cheese, sauces, bouillon, or lemon juice can make ordinary canned food more palatable.

Appropriate beverages are served with meals. Juice accom-panies breakfast with a choice of cocoa (and powdered or long-life milk), coffee, tea, or fresh milk; for lunch fruit juice, beer, or milk; for dinner wine, beer, fruit juice, or milk. Milk can be purchased daily everywhere or long-life milk can be carried.

Fruit is available for both lunch and dinner with occasional pastries, cookies, or other treat for dessert. We usually served vegetables for dinner because it was more convenient to pull out the sandwiches we had made in the morning for lunch on the road. Soup as a first course for dinner is relaxing while the rest of the dinner cooks. Then the soup pot can be filled with water and heated during the meal for dishwashing.

On days when a "rolling breakfast" is desirable to get going, there is canned juice, fruit, hard cheese, rolls, and other easily eaten food that can be served with no preparation. Car coffee pots are available that can be plugged into the cigarette lighter. By boiling water and supplying instant mixes, it is possible to stretch out breakfast over half the morning.

These menus do not involve foods that take long to heat, or that require more than opening cans and combining. If you want to increase cooking time and fuel consumption, there are all sorts of pasta and rice dishes to try.

We chose not to carry anything that we did not consider easily transportable. For example, we did not carry cooking oil but in-stead used a little margarine in our Teflon pan. Except for fruit, which we purchased in markets frequently, we did not carry foods that bruised easily. We did buy fresh meat occasionally, when it happened to be convenient, but did not carry it. Traveling with a cooler, as we do in the United States, did not seem necessary.

Not all foods that you are familiar with will be available everywhere. It is a matter of searching for products in the supermarket of your choice for the increasing variety of freeze-dried, dehydrated, or canned foods to try. You may want to stock up a little when you find a good source.

	Breakfast	Lunch	Dinner
Day 1	French toast sausage	tuna sandwiches	onion soup sherried ham/ pineapple* potato salad
Day 2	scrambled eggs bacon rolls	bacon sandwiches (make extra at breakfast)	consomme sausages/cabbage* new potatoes Waldorf salad
Day 3	Familia (hot cereal with dried fruit) hard cheese/apple	free choice (bread, crackers, peanut butter, jelly, cheese, meat spread)	tomato soup spaghetti/meatballs* mixed vegetables cole slaw
Day 4	pancakes bacon	salami/cheese sandwiches	chicken broth paella* cucumber salad
Day 5	fried eggs corned beef hash	deviled ham sandwiches	split pea soup tuna oriental* carrot/raisin salad
Day 6	fried potatoes Spam	ham/cheese sandwiches	madrilene beef stroganoff* lettuce/tomato salad
Day 7	cheese omelet sausage	free choice	mushroom soup chicken curry* mixed vegetable salad

*recipe given below

Dinner Recipes

APPETIZERS   Many European shops carry quite a variety of exotic or ordinary treats in tubes, from caviar or shrimp to mayonnaise. Cheese, meat, seafood spreads, or other surprises may be tried on crackers. The wonderful realm of cheeses available in great variety in each country is tempting to explore. We had our cheeseboard in operation before dinner many nights as well as at lunch. Sometimes we would make an antipasto using whatever we had on hand—salami, cheese, anchovies, celery, olives, sardines, tuna, beans, and the like.

BACON

BACON HASH (serves 4)
6 slices bacon, diced
2 cans sliced potatoes, 16 oz each
1 onion, diced
Fry bacon and onion. Add potatoes and heat.

BACON/BAKED BEANS (serves 4)
2 cans baked beans
6 slices bacon, diced
½ pkg. onion soup mix
½ cup catsup
2 t marmalade
Fry bacon. Add rest and simmer.

BEEF

BEEF STROGANOFF (serves 4)
1 can roast beef, cubed, 12 oz
1 can onions, 15½ oz
1 can mushrooms, 4 oz
1 can mushroom soup
1 pkg sour cream mix, reconstituted
salt and pepper
dill
Heat all except sour cream. Add just before serving. Serve over instant rice or noodles.

TIP

Serve creamed dishes over potato cakes (made from instant potatoes), rice, noodles, English muffins, toast, Chinese noodles, shoestring potatoes, crushed potato chips.

CAMPSITE STEW (serves 4)
1 can roast beef (or meatballs)
1 can onions, 15½ oz
1 can cream-style corn or carrots, 16 oz
1 can potatoes, 16 oz
salt and pepper
Heat. Serve with chunk of French bread.

SPAGHETTI AND MEATBALLS (serves 6–8)
8 oz Spaghetti
1 t salt
1 can mushrooms, 4 oz
1 can meatballs
½ c milk, water, or wine
2 pkgs sour cream, reconstituted
2 t parsley
2 T Parmesan cheese
Cook spaghetti. Add rest and heat. Serve immediately
or add liquid.

SLOPPY JOES (serves 4)
1 can ground beef
1 can chicken gumbo or minestrone soup
2 T mustard
4 T catsup
½ t Worcestershire sauce
½ t salt
1 can tomato soup
Heat. Serve on buns.

TIP

Add 1 can chili instead of chicken gumbo or minestrone
soup to make chili burgers.

SPANISH RICE (serves 4)
1 c rice
1 c onion, diced
½ c green pepper, diced
2 T oil or margarine
1 can ground beef

1 can tomato sauce, 15 oz
1½ c boiling water
½ t salt, dash of pepper
Sauté rice, onion, pepper, and beef in oil. Add rest and bring to boil. Simmer until done.

CHEESE

CHEESE RAREBIT (serves 4)
½ lb grated Cheddar or other hard cheese
1 can tomato soup
½ c water or beer
1 t Worcestershire sauce
½ t salt
1 egg
Combine all except egg. Heat and melt cheese. Add beaten egg. Stir until thickened. Dip chunks of French bread in rarebit or serve on toast.

CHEESE FONDUE (serves 4)
½ lb. shredded Swiss cheese
1½ T flour
1 c dry white wine
salt, pepper, nutmeg
Dredge cheese with flour, salt, pepper, nutmeg. Heat wine. When air bubbles rise to surface add cheese by handfuls, stirring until dissolved. Dip chunks of French bread in fondue.

CHICKEN

CHICKEN CURRY (serves 4–6)
1 can chicken, 5 oz
1 apple, cubed
1 onion, diced
½ c raisins
½ T curry powder
1 T lemon peel
½ t ginger
1 can chicken broth
½ c dry milk
1 c instant rice

Sauté onion and apple. Add rest and heat. Simmer 5 minutes. Pass curry condiments such as chutney, chopped nuts, grated coconut.

COQ AU VIN (serves 4)
1 can chicken, 5 oz
1 can onions, 15½ oz
1 can mushrooms, 4 oz
1 can mushroom soup
½ t salt
dash of pepper
parsley
½ c white wine
Heat. May add sliced water chestnuts or slivered almonds. Serve with rice.

HAWAIIAN CHICKEN (serves 4–6)
1 can chicken, 5 oz
½ c white wine
1 can water chestnuts, sliced, 5 oz
1 can mushrooms, 4 oz
1 can pineapple chunks, drained, 5¼ oz
2 T flour
½ t salt
½ c raisins
4 green onions
Sauté onions. Blend in flour and salt. Add wine, cook until thickened. Add rest and heat. Serve over rice.

CHICKEN WITH GREEN BEANS (serves 4)
1 can chicken, 5 oz
1 can green beans, 16 oz
1 can mushroom soup
1 can mushrooms, 4 oz
Heat. Serve over Chinese noodles. May add 1 can French-fried onions.

CORNED BEEF

CORNED BEEF BOILED DINNER (serves 4–6)
1 t salt
½ t pepper

1 t caraway seed
1 can potatoes, 16 oz
1 can carrots, 16 oz
1 onion
½ head cabbage
1 can corned beef, 12 oz
½ t parsley

Heat salt, caraway seed, potatoes and carrots un-drained. Push to edge of skillet and add chopped cabbage. Cook 5 minutes. Add cubed beef and parsley. Heat through. Serve with chunks of French bread.

CORNED BEEF HASH WITH EGGS (serves 4)
1 can corned beef hash, 15 oz
4 eggs

Divide hash into 4 patties. Fry one side, turn, make a dent with a spoon. Break an egg into each dent and cook until done.

HAM (OR SPAM)   SHERRIED HAM (serves 4)
1 small canned ham, 24 oz
1 can pineapple rings, drained, 5¼ oz
2 T sherry

Slice ham. Add juices from can. Add drained pineapple. Heat. Add sherry before serving.

HAM WITH POTATO PATTIES (serves 4)
1⅓ c instant potatoes
½ t salt
2 T butter or margarine
⅔ c dry milk
1⅓ c water
1 can ham, sliced
¼ lb Cheddar cheese

Heat water, milk, butter, and salt. Stir in instant potatoes. May need a little more liquid. Form patties and fry, add cheese and turn. Heat ham slices.

SPAM SPANISH RICE (serves 4)
1 can Spam, cubed
1 onion
1½ cups instant rice
1 pkg spaghetti sauce mix
2 c water
Sauté onion and Spam. Add rest and heat.

SPAM AND MACARONI (serves 4)
1 can Spam, cubed
2 cans macaroni and cheese
½ c milk
½ t salt
1 t onion flakes
Mix and heat.

SPAM WITH OLIVES (serves 4)
1 can Spam, in strips
1 can onion soup
1 c water
1⅓ c instant rice
2 T parsley
10 stuffed olives, sliced
Sauté ham strips. Stir in water. Add rice, onion soup,
parsley, and olives, Heat and serve.

HOT DOGS

HOT DOGS/BAKED BEANS (serves 4)
1 can hot dogs
2 cans baked beans
½ pkg onion soup mix
½ c catsup
Heat baked beans. Cut up hot dogs and add. Heat.

HOT DOGS AU GRATIN (serves 4)
1 can hot dogs
1 can cheese soup
1 can potatoes
Heat and eat.

HOT DOGS/SAUERKRAUT (serves 4)
1 can hot dogs
1 can sauerkraut
Heat hot dogs in sauerkraut. Serve with chunks of French bread.

RICE

BASIC INSTANT RICE RECIPE
1 can soup
1¾ c hot water
1 c vegetables
1 c meat, poultry, or seafood
Add 1⅓ c rice to soup mixture. Simmer 5 minutes. May garnish with French-fried onions.

TIP

When cooking rice you may include bouillon cubes, onion soup mix, tomato soup, mushroom soup, celery soup, cheese soup, sautéed onion, dill, parsley, tarragon, or other herbs for flavor.

SAUSAGES

SAUSAGES/CABBAGE (serves 4–6)
2 cans Vienna sausage, 5 oz each
1 cabbage
2 apples
1 t caraway seed
½ t dill
Chop and cook cabbage in water. Add rest and simmer until heated.

SEAFOOD

PAELLA (serves 8)
1 can tuna, 6½ oz
1 can shrimp, 4½ oz
1 can mushrooms, 4 oz
1 onion
1⅓ c rice (instant)
1¾ c water
1 can Vienna sausage, 5 oz
1 can chicken, 5 oz
1 t salt

½ t pepper
Heat water. Add rest and simmer until rice is done.

ORIENTAL SEAFOOD (serves 4–6)
1 onion
2 stalks celery
1 can celery soup
1 can chop suey vegetables, undrained
1 can shrimp, 4½ oz
Heat. May add slivered almonds or ground ginger.
Serve over Chinese noodles.

CRAB CAKES (serves 4)
1 can crabmeat, 6½ oz
2 eggs, beaten
1 c bread crumbs or cubes
1 t Worcestershire sauce
½ t dry mustard
1 T parsley
½ t salt
dash of pepper
water to moisten
Form into patties and fry. Serve with tartar sauce.

SKILLET TUNA (serves 4)
1 can tuna, 6½ oz
1 can mushroom soup
½ c milk
½ c grated Cheddar cheese
1½ c instant rice
dash of pepper
1 can whole tomatoes
1 cup water
1 t onion flakes
10 sliced olives
Heat water. Add rest and simmer 5 minutes.

TUNA ORIENTAL (serves 6–8)
4 eggs, beaten
1 can tuna 6½ oz
1 can mushrooms, 4 oz
1 can bean sprouts, drained
2 green onions, chopped
2 stalks celery, chopped
salt, pepper
2 t soy sauce
Mix and fry as pancakes. Serve with rice.

SOUP

BERGEN SOUP
1 can green pea soup
1 pkg sour cream, reconstituted
1 can hot dogs, sliced
1 T dill
½ c water
½ t salt
dash of pepper
Heat.

CABBAGE CHOWDER
1 can meatballs
1 onion
1 small chopped cabbage
½ t salt
1 can celery soup
¼ c dry milk
2 c water
½ c instant potatoes
Sauté onion, cabbage. Add rest and simmer.

CHEESE BISQUE
1 can cheese soup
1 c milk
⅓ c sherry
Heat. Add sherry just before serving.

CORN CHOWDER
1 pkg leek soup
⅔ c dry milk
2 cans water
1 can corn
½ c instant potatoes
¼ lb shredded cheese
1 T salt
dash of pepper
Heat.

CRAB BISQUE
1 stalk chopped celery
1 can crab
1 can mushrooms
⅔ c dry milk
2 cans water
1 t Worcestershire sauce
Heat.

SEAFOOD CHOWDER
1 can tomato soup
1 can mushroom soup
1½ c milk
1 can sliced potatoes
1 can tuna
1 can crab
2 T onion flakes
½ c instant potatoes
Heat.

WELSH SOUP
1 can cheese soup
1 can beer
½ c milk
1 c grated Cheddar cheese
1 t salt
½ t pepper
Heat.

TIPS

Save liquid in vegetable cans for soup the same night.

Add instant mashed potatoes to thicken soup for chowder.

Add croutons to soup for interest.

Add dumplings by mixing 1 c biscuit mix, ¼ c dry milk, ⅓ c water. Drop in hot soup. Cook 20 minutes.

Make dumplings with corn muffin mix. May also add herbs.

Garnish soup with a dollop of sour cream, sprinkling of chives, lemon slice, parsley, crushed potato chips, popcorn, pretzel, bacon bits, green peppers, grated cheese, slivered almonds, or mushroom slices.

VEGETABLES

Good combinations include:
Asparagus with cheese sauce, or with Parmesan cheese and nutmeg
Green beans—with bean sprouts, mushrooms, soy sauce, cheese sauce, and/or water chestnuts
Beets—with orange juice and peel, with vinegar, or marmalade; or with honey, brown sugar, or ginger mixed with orange juice
Cabbage—with white sauce or cheese sauce, or celery soup with soy sauce, or bacon bits
Carrots—with basil, marjoram, onions, apple juice, lemon juice; or brown sugar or ginger and orange juice
Onions—with peanuts, white sauce or celery soup, grated cheese or peas, mushroom soup
Peas —with mint jelly, onions, or peppers
Potatoes—with cheese soup, or onions, mushrooms, thyme, marjoram, dill, lemon, or chives
Tomatoes—with onions, mushrooms, or ginger

TIPS

Reconstitute freeze-dried vegetables by using vinegar or lemon juice in the water.

Add any of the following to canned vegetables: horse-radish, grated cheese, crumbs, green peppers, onions, celery, water chestnuts, almonds, sour cream, bouillon, bacon, herbs, cheese sauce, bacon bits, ginger, orange juice.

PAYING

Comparative Food Costs

We discovered again the startling disparity in food costs as we traveled from country to country in 1977. Unless we really *believed* what we knew to be true—that prices in one country may be double those in another—a trip through a supermarket could be depressing. The subsequent slide in the value of the dollar in Europe will make all food more expensive for Americans, but particularly in countries with very strong currency, like Germany and Switzerland. Sometimes we scrapped our preplanned menus and started over if we could not find what we needed at reasonable prices; at other times we threw caution to the winds and bought as people on holiday like to buy.

Because we were living in England for a year we were able to get to know which stores carried meatballs in a tasty sauce; or a combination of hamburger patties and sausages in a can (Ranch Grill made by Danoxa); canned salads including potato, cabbage, cucumber, and mixed vegetables, and a wide variety of meat spreads. For each trip we purchased more cans than we needed. We counted the cans that were left at the end of the trip by contents and then knew which foods the family enjoyed most. This also gave us an estimate for meals for the next trip. We have since found that the variety of tasty meats and salads available in cans is much smaller in the United States than in Europe, perhaps because Europeans do not have the mammoth refrigerators we do and therefore need to have a supply of food in cans. Most refrigerators in England are about the size of a dishwasher, and freezers are not widely used.

SAMPLE MENU FOR A PARTY OF FOUR*

		England	France	Germany	Italy	Belgium	Holland	Norway
Breakfast	Bread (½ loaf)	$ .14	$ .21	$ .49	$ .33	$ .39	$ .38	$ .34
	Milk (1 pint)	.18	.20	.16	.21	.38	.21	.15
	Eggs (4)	.47	.77	.80	.45	.77	.40	.72
	Juice	.36	.30	.57	.33	.86	.32	.45
		$1.15	$1.48	$2.02	$1.32	$ 2.40	$1.31	$ 1.66
Lunch	Bread (½ loaf)	$ .14	$ .21	$ .49	$ .33	$ .39	$ .38	$ .34
	Cheese (8 oz.)	.93	.91	.94	.97	.79	1.15	1.33
	Oranges (4)	.35	.44	.23	.26	.45	.20	.59
	Wine (½ bottle)	.85	.76	, .97	.68	.63	.65	2.00
	Milk (1 pint)	.18	.20	.16	.21	.38	.21	.15
		$2.45	$2.52	$2.79	$2.45	$ 2.64	$2.59	$ 4.41
Dinner	Ham (small can)	$1.28	$1.80	$1.14	$1.50	$ 1.83	$1.72	$ 4.90
	Pineapple (20 oz.)	.54	.98	.59	.50	.98	.81	1.17
	Green beans (16 oz.)	.29	.61	.50	.40	.29	.81	1.29
	Wine (½ bottle)	.85	.76	.97	.68	.63	.65	2.00
	Juice	.36	.30	.57	.33	.86	.32	.45
	Cookies	.20	.65	.82	.34	.64	.86	1.04
		$3.52	$5.10	$4.59	$3.75	$ 5.23	$5.17	$10.85
	Totals for one day	$7.12	$9.10	$9.40	$7.52	$10.27	$9.07	$16.92

*1977 prices converted to dollars. Prices have risen since 1977, but the table can still be used to estimate relative costs. What has most affected these prices since 1977 is the decline in relative value of the dollar.

We planned a sample menu for one day for a family of two adults and two teenaged children and shopped in each of seven countries for it. We picked large supermarkets with prices available where one of us could browse with notebook in hand while the rest of the family did the other shopping. There were some problems in controlling the comparison: for example, it was difficult to find a small canned ham of similar quality everywhere. Wine varied greatly, even though we tried to pick the low end of the price range, and we sometimes had beer or juice rather than wine with lunch. Our children chose juice or "squash" (a fruit drink in England) when milk was not available at noon. The menu does not include a salad because we could not always find good lettuce; in fact, we did have salad every night, usually the excellent canned salads from England. We did use staples such as coffee and marmalade that are not listed. The sample menu is not entirely complete, but it is constant from country to country and should be helpful in estimating relative food costs for party of four.

Avoiding Campsite Inflation

Many campgrounds have stores on the grounds. They are very handy for a forgotten item or two, but the supplies are usually limited and rather expensive. Often fresh bread, rolls, or croissants are available in the morning at the camp store, and we did indulge ourselves in these local luxuries. We also usually purchased milk there every morning so we could have it cold. Sometimes it was even delivered to the tent! In one area there was a farm on the grounds, and the fresh eggs we bought there all had double yolks and were of giant size.

Campsite fees vary widely according to the amenities offered and the season of the year. Resort locations charge much higher fees because campers are a captive group when they choose to vacation there. We often camped off-season and were usually charged less than the standard rate if we "opened" the campground. The manager often apologized for the hastily cleaned bathrooms and hoped we would enjoy our stay. Those that offered only the barest necessities did not charge very much, and often the superb view of a lakeside meadow or the fun of living within the grounds of a ruined castle made it all worthwhile. During holiday seasons (for example, Easter in Italy, Whitsun in England, August in France) in resort areas the campgrounds were jammed with tourists who paid very high fees indeed. It didn't pay to shop around at such seasons in desirable resort areas because all decent camping areas were charging high fees. Some campgrounds offered a discount for those carrying "camping carnets." The other reason to carry a camping carnet is even more important: the campground manager will usually hold it instead of your passport until you check out and pay your bill. We did not feel completely easy about giving up a passport to a campsite clerk and also sometimes needed it during the day to cash traveler's checks.

Campground charges are set on various bases—the vehicle, tent or tents, dining canopy or tent extension, or number of campers. Some charge by the person, others charge by the size of each tent. For those with caravans there is an additional charge for electrical hookup. Our entourage included one car, one large tent with extension, two small tents, and four persons. We paid anywhere from $1.05 to $9.17 per night, depending upon location and season. During a trip to Italy we paid a low of $2.40 in a gorgeous campsite on Lake Como not yet fully opened and a high of $9.17 a week later at Sorrento on Easter weekend. Most campsite guides list prices, but such listings are often out of date and may be inapplicable during the season in which you arrive. It is a good idea to check the posted prices at a campground when you arrive (including local taxes and extra fees) to be sure of the cost. But no matter what the specific cost at a site, remember that it is likely to be only 10% to 20% of what it would cost to put your party up in a pension or hotel for the night.

How to Keep Money in Your Pocket

With the uncertain fluctuation of the dollar it is difficult to predict your costs accurately, but it still pays to *plan* to get the most pleasure for the least money. Traveling by camping is a good start in European economies because normal lodging and ordinary meals have soared out of sight. The night we arrived, when we were not yet set up for camping, cost us nearly as much as a ten-day trip later in the fall: $45 for a single tiny room for four and $20 more for a very simple meal. At that rate, adding in two other meals and incidentals, our family would have spent a minimum of $80 per day, or $560 per week, without any extras. No camping trip we took even approached such a figure. Camping keeps your budget from being wasted on food and lodging, freeing you to spend your money elsewhere.

There are other economies which help to make a trip inexpensive as well as enjoyable. The fares to Europe have now dropped enough to offset higher prices for food and goods. You can plan shorter visits in countries that are the most expensive, camping just over the border in a less expensive country and taking day trips back and forth. You can plan ahead to buy gasoline coupons where they are available (particularly important in Italy). You can buy small things to remember pleasant days instead of stocking up on sweaters and other items that are no longer much of a bargain in Europe. You can plan to take advantage of the free sightseeing available almost everywhere; there is a great deal of natural beauty to enjoy; hiking, open-air festivals, cathedrals, visits to charming little villages with half-timbered buildings are all free. Even in cities, there are many things you can do that do not cost much—you can spend all day in the Louvre or the British Museum for a small entrance fee.

To see just how cheaply we could travel, we planned a ten-day trip through central Wales, Snowdonia in northern Wales and the Lake District in England. The total cost for four people for ten days was $88. (This did not count the canned goods we brought from home but did include gas, fish and chips "out" twice, campground fees, and miscellaneous expenses.) We lived quite simply and found we could enjoy it that way; on succeeding trips we did not feel obliged to live so austerely. Our most expensive trip, a twenty-four-day trip through Germany, Switzerland, Italy, and Belgium, cost us $843, including everything but our canned goods from England (see page 12). We camped only thirteen nights because we stayed with relatives and friends the other eight nights.

Another trip, taken in January, 1977, does not belong in this book, but it does provide an instructive comparison. We chose not to camp but to stay in hotels for five nights, and we also rented an apartment for one week. With the addition of ski rental, lift tickets, and more meals out en route our cost was a whopping $1,261. (Again, this did not include canned goods for the week in the apartment.) This trip reinforced our desire to travel by camping whenever possible. With warm sleeping bags we could have camped with reasonable comfort, even in January. There are campgrounds open all year round in or near most major cities and in mountain valleys near ski areas throughout the Alps. It would be wise to study temperature and precipitation charts for any area before undertaking tent camping during the winter, but caravan camping should be possible in any region in which you can manage winter roads.

GETTING HELP WHEN YOU NEED IT

Although we have not yet had to seek emergency help in our travels, it could happen. Any problems encountered by a traveler can be upsetting, but inconvenience should not ruin the trip. There may be different kinds of solutions in various countries. In any case, there *are* solutions.

Getting Bumped From a Flight

To avoid getting bumped, plan to arrive at the airport early. Allow plenty of time to check in and get to the gate. On flights originating in the United States, airlines must pay "denied boarding compensation" to anyone who is bumped. The carrier must immediately furnish you with a written explanation of the terms, conditions, and limitations of the compensation. And the carrier must schedule you on a flight to arrive at your destination within four hours of your scheduled arrival.

Before you go, write to the Consumer Information Center, Pueblo, Colorado for two publications entitled *Air Travelers' Fly-Rights* and *Consumer Guide to International Air Travel.* If you cannot settle satisfactorily with an airline after having been bumped, you can send complaints to Office of Consumer Affairs, Civil Aeronautics Board, 1825 Connecticut Avenue N.W., Washington, D.C. 20428. The office will not adjudicate claims but can advise you on the best procedure to follow.

Losing Your Passport

Report the loss of your passport to the local police. Then contact the nearest American embassy or consulate, which will issue a replacement. It is helpful to carry two extra passport photos, the number, date, and place of issue of your passport, and some other form of identification separately. If you cannot adequately establish your identity and citizenship, the embassy or consulate will have to cable or telex the State Department for instructions, which may cause some delay.

Losing Your Traveler's Checks

Either the nearest office or bank that deals with the issuing authority of your traveler's checks can reimburse you with checks for those you've lost. It pays to keep the purchase information and numbers of your checks in a separate, safe place while traveling. If you need further help, the nearest American embassy or consulate can advise you on the procedure to follow. They can also help you, *in a real emergency*, to get in touch with bankers, employers, or friends in order to get needed funds. Someone at home can cable money abroad in 24 to 48 hours.

Resolving Medical Problems

The American embassy or consulate will help you find appropriate medical services, including English-speaking physicians. We have found that people on the spot have been able to advise us when we needed quick medical service. A sprained ankle in Zermatt turned into a more pleasant experience than we had expected, with several days of going about in a horse-drawn sleigh to visit a jovial Swiss doctor who laughed and joked during each heat treatment, and rides up in the chairlift (with crutches instead of skis) to enjoy a gorgeous view. In England we signed on at the local surgery (National Health Service), and were seen much more quickly than we would have been in the United States. In case of a severe emergency, when medical evacuation is necessary, you can call (202) 632-3529 in Washington, D. C. to reach the office of special consular services; during the night and weekends, call (202) 655-4000.

State Department officials suggest that travelers take some precautions such as carrying extra money in the form of traveler's checks, leaving a copy of your itinerary with a relative or friend, and carrying an identification card for any health insurance coverage that embraces foreign travel.

Encountering the Law

You should know that most European countries strictly enforce traffic laws. One of the real advantages of belonging to an automobile club is the service it will render if you do get into trouble. In case of an accident, follow the same procedure that you would at home, beginning with getting medical aid for the injured. In most countries you must carry and display a warning triangle to warn traffic of an obstruction. You must notify the police if it is a statutory requirement of the country, if someone is injured or dead, or if there is no one present to represent the injured.

ENJOYING

With Children

Some children hate a trip that is heavily loaded with art galleries, cathedrals, and museums and vow not to enjoy any of it. Involving them in some of the conversations before the plan is established and letting them help choose among desirable options can go a long way toward insuring their enjoyment of the trip. Without too much effort you can do a little research on the countries you will visit and the attractions you might choose to see. There are endless literary works to enjoy before going. Some families choose to seek out a special interest, such as visiting every Van Gogh museum in Holland. The British Museum has enough variety to reach some special interest your child has developed in school, whether it be Egyptian mummies or ancient coins. Those with marine interests will find famous ships and many kinds of boats preserved in maritime museums scattered throughout European ports. There is a wealth of music to listen to in especially interesting surroundings, like the King's College Choir in Cambridge or the Vienna Boys' Choir, as well as many concerts and performances of opera and ballet in major cities. Famous ancient buildings and ruins can be enjoyed in depth by anyone, and country houses, castles, and cathedrals abound.

Collecting

Many people enjoy collecting something while they travel. The range is limitless: postcards, maps, decals, recipes, foreign stamps, fabric badges to sew on backpacks, demitasse spoons, recipe books, traditional costumes, tiles to make into a coffee table at home, and other souvenir items. Usually everyone in our family is collecting something different on a trip. As long as the items are not too bulky or too hard to procure, collecting can be fun—and if there are children in your party, you'll find that the collecting impulse can even make that perennial adult interest—shopping—more tolerable for them.

Keeping a Journal

It's easy to acquire the habit of writing in a journal every day on a camping trip. Even children can develop their own styles and fresh points of view, which often differ remarkably from those of their parents. Wherever we have traveled we have bought several postcards to paste in the journals opposite the narrative, adding zip and interest to the books. As our children walked through art galleries for example, they thought about their favorite works and hoped to find postcards of those for their books. We have enjoyed seeing Europe through their eyes and we have all read and reread their journals as well as our own to recapture an exciting part of past travels. Through journals, parents can pick up clues to their children's enjoyment of activities during the trip. You may not have known that your child had always wanted to see the Mona Lisa and was delighted to take her picture home to hang on a bedroom wall. We have enjoyed reading a description of the details learned while exploring the *Wasa*, a ship raised from the bottom of Stockholm harbor, from the eyes of one of our children.

Balancing Tourism and Sports

Breaking the customary pattern of sightseeing can boost travelers' morale. You can intersperse touring with sports having a special appeal, such as glacier walking in Norway or Switzerland, hiking in the English Lake District, or cycling in Holland. Swimming is available in lakes and in pools, as well as fjords (sometimes cold) and fine ocean beaches. You can charter a sailboat for a day on a beautiful lake or along the coast. You can go to an English game of soccer or cricket, watch the regatta at Henley, lawn tennis at Wimbledon, or horse racing at Ascot. Most national tourist bureaus can send you a detailed schedule of special sports events in advance.

Choosing What to Do

Lists of museums, art galleries, castles, and cathedrals are available from tourist offices and from guidebooks as well. Some of them are free, some ask a modest admission fee or a donation, some are more expensive. On the whole, admission fees are not a major cost on a trip and they do help to support the maintenance of what you came to see. You will need to decide which to visit with the interests of your group in mind. It is not easy to choose when so much is offered, but some of what you might do can always be saved for another trip. The rule of thumb is not to be compulsive about seeing *everything*.

Finding Local Sights

Save time for attractions that you hear about when you are actually there. Local people always know about something the rest of the world has not heard about. You may find a little church that has a collection of paintings of ships done by the men who sailed them long ago, as we did in Italy. You may meet someone who wants to show you a building that means a great deal to his family. You may have a friend who can show you a little town not yet on the tourist trail where the inhabitants wear their traditional dress all the time. You may encounter another hiker who has found a trail off the beaten path with a gorgeous view. Sometimes, local surprises mean a great deal more than following the customary tourist route to "major" attractions.

RELAXING

Compulsiveness is a demon that is very hard to lick. Most people overplan because they cannot bear to give up even part of what they might do. The more places we read about, the more we want to experience. The more we meet people and talk about their interests and impressions, the more we want to share those too. We *know* we will be tired and cranky if we drive too many hours, traipse through too many long hallways, and go at a rapid pace from one thing to another all day long. The problem is then to choose—to choose what will be pleasing to us and yet not too arduous. The rule is never too much or too long.

Time Out for Everyone

There will be times on a trip when you won't want to go along on an outing that the other member or members of your group are eager to try. You shouldn't have to. Perhaps you have some letterwriting to do, or want a chance to sit by the tent and do needlepoint while absorbing the sunshine and the view. If you are bored by too much shopping, you can choose something else you want to do while the others plough through the Straw Market in Florence. You may want to continue looking at favorite paintings while the other has "had it," so you can separate and regroup later.

Everyone needs relief from togetherness on a trip; if you get some time alone you can rejoin the group later, refreshed.

Discovering a Mediterranean Sense of Time

Relax and enjoy. The people who live around and near the Mediterranean have a beautiful life. They live in spectacular settings and they know how to relax and enjoy each day. They can work hard building up their stone fences for their children and grandchildren; they can be outside all day cultivating and improving their land. But on a special day when the mood is right, they put a sign on the door of their business and take a young son out fishing. They can sit in the square in mid-morning, drinking coffee and enjoying their friends. They can drop everything when you come to call and offer an aperitif or coffee for an hour of conversation. We have vowed that we will try to remember and relax when we return to the United States, but it is not easy to import this sense of living into American culture.

A trip can be a perfect time to try to relax and enjoy your family. No one has to set an alarm and get to a job on time. No one has routine tasks to perform, apart from those of keeping camp. You can take time out for a child, a view, a new friend, a new experience—if you will.

4

suggested itineraries

The following trips will bring campers into some of the most interesting areas of Europe; each has variety in terrain and activity. All have been designed for campers who want to balance the greatest possible enjoyment with economy. Every itinerary includes a suggested pattern for the trip, details of routing, mileage, a map, sightseeing tips, and sources of other information on the areas to be visited. Each plan outlines a specific trip that has worked well for family camping, but the locality, length, and pattern of activity can easily be modified to plan similar trips for singles, couples, or other small groups.

The **Southwestern Circuit** includes exploration along the south coast of England with plenty of exposure to Britain's great maritime tradition, early Roman civilization, and some of the wildest moors in the country. A number of splendid cathedrals lie on or near the route, and there is plenty of opportunity for walking along rugged coasts and through lovely villages and college towns.

The **Central Circuit** will appeal especially to hikers and climbers, although it also offers short strolls at historic sites or amid scenes of extraordinary natural beauty. Those with a compelling interest in Shakespeare or in castles will have more than enough to explore. The wild terrain of the Snowdonia region of Wales is matched by the meshing of water and mountains in the Lake District of England. Oxford and Cambridge, ancient college towns, lie at the beginning and end of this trip.

Scotland has a fascination all its own in rich historical and romantic legends and a bold landscape full of sharp contrasts. Sportsmen will find excellent fishing, hiking, and climbing, as well as swimming and boating in resort beach areas.

Scandinavia offers a spectacular collage of land and water with natural beauty everywhere. Scenery in Denmark, Sweden, and Norway ranges from mountains, glaciers, and fjords to rolling hills and farmland near the lakes. Cities are full of interesting modern and ancient architecture, with superb shopping an added attraction. Local traditions, crafts, and festivals abound in every region.

Central Europe is by far the most ambitious adventure. The range of possible layovers, cultural attractions, natural beauty, and opportunities for special interests or sports is wide. The suggested itinerary includes sites of special historical interest in Holland, France, Switzerland, Italy, Austria, and Germany, and spectacular mountain and seaside landscapes.

THE SOUTHWESTERN CIRCUIT (ENGLAND)

From London: Hampshire, Isle of Wight, Dorset, Devon, Bath, Stonehenge, Oxford
(10 days: 572 miles/915 kilometers)

This trip provides a balance between the exploration of history and the sheer relaxation and pleasure of enjoying life in seaside towns, with many evenings spent amidst quiet scenes of beauty rather than in the noise and excitement of large cities. The route has been planned to allow brief stopovers at points of interest on the way to a destination and longer stays for more intensive exploration in areas of special beauty or interest. There are a number of side trips and hikes you can take without moving camp. Children will enjoy Lord Nelson's flagship, the H.M.S. *Victory,* and the Maritime Museum in **Exeter**. The ferry to the **Isle of Wight** gives marvelous views of all sorts of ships and yachts in the harbors. In **Salcombe** you can hike along spectacular cliffs or enjoy beaches. **Stonehenge** will fascinate those who wonder about the ordeal of assembling such huge stones and the reason for the symmetrical arrangement.

The itinerary includes a number of England's most interesting cathedrals, splendid with soaring spires and stained-glass windows. Both the sad-eyed ponies and the prison on **Dartmoor** impart a gloom that sets off the expanse and isolation of the moor. There are a number of Roman villas in varying stages of excavation; one in the **Chichester** area has exquisite mosaic floors. Chichester is a marvelous area for sailors; you can charter cruising boats or daysailers for poking around harbors. **Salisbury** and **Winchester** cathedrals are within easy reach of this area. The rolling **Cotswolds**, dotted with sheep, unfold the lives of the wool merchants who lived there. Memorials to them can be found in churches in the form of brass plates elaborately engraved with figures, sheep, dogs, epigraphs, and ornate canopies. The imprint

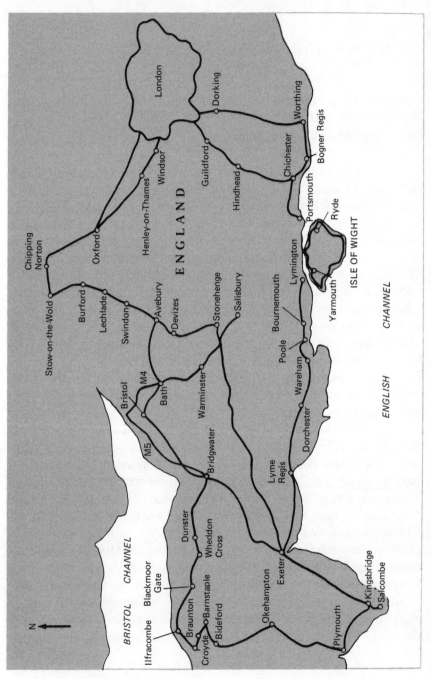

from brasses can be rubbed on paper with a wax crayon and taken home to be framed. **Oxford**, with its many enclosed colleges and pleasant gardens, needs a day of exploration on foot for the visitor to discover its charms. Those who follow this itinerary have many choices of activity and will find it difficult to leave something for the next trip.

The *cost* of this trip is not excessive for several reasons. Mileage is limited by the fact that the same roads that provide striking views are often narrow and curvy and do not encourage one to drive much over 30 miles per hour. Some of the roads have only one lane, some are also footpaths for sheep, and some have high hedgerows loaded with primroses. Beauty is abundant, and travelers are relaxed and cordial about backing up to a passing place on one-lane roads.

Food costs can be kept low by shopping as the British do. Most housewives shop each day, buying fresh fruits, vegetables, and meats in small quantities. You can stock up on canned goods and staples in a supermarket and then enjoy the fun of buying fresh provisions in smaller shops or in open markets. You will discover the specialities of each region from the people who live there as well as from fellow campers. Word passes fast when crab is available in Salcombe; you can often get fresh bread still warm and fragrant from a village bakery, or fish and chips piping hot and wrapped in newspaper. Most English towns have a market day at least once a week, and it is fun to wander among the open stalls savoring special cheeses, fruits, and vegetables, and snooping for household bargains of all kinds. The vendors hawking their wares add good humor to the atmosphere, as long as you don't mind being called "Ducky" or "Love."

Campground costs are lower in England than on the Continent. The facilities are not as elaborate, and in some cases can be quite primitive. However, there is some appeal in sharing ground with the ghosts of the past near a partly ruined old castle, or being in a meadow with cows and sheep that may occasionally peer into your tent. On the other hand, when a hot shower/white sinks/formica counters combination seems like a dream, you can find it.

*Entrance fees** for castles and museums range from $.40 to $1.21. There are three kinds of control over the many magnificent historic properties in England: the Department of the Environment, the National Trust, and private ownership. Travelers who expect to be in England for some time may save money by purchasing admission cards from the Department of the Environment for $2.71 each. Membership is available at any of the historic sites or from The Secretary, Department of the Environment, Room 106, 25 Savile Row, London, W.1. The National Trust also offers membership for $15.00; this is available from Miss Arete B. Swartz, Executive Director, Royal Oak Foundation, Inc., 41 East 72nd Street, New York, N.Y. 10021. A brochure listing all the country houses, abbeys, castles, and gardens that may be enjoyed by showing the card contains other useful information about opening and closing dates and times. In addition, a guide entitled *Historic Houses, Castles, and Gardens* (ABC Historic Publications, Oldhill, London Road, Dunstable, Bedfordshire), available in most book shops, also lists those properties that are still privately owned but open to the public.

Other expenses will probably include some meals out. A delicious pub lunch usually costs under $1.00 and can be enjoyed in a setting of polished paneling, surrounded by collections of brass and copper hanging from the ceiling. Menu selections range from a hearty "plowman's lunch," chicken, shrimp or fish with chips, salads, and scotch eggs, to a complete buffet. Fish and chips, bought hot and shared in a park or on a beach, are a treat for children, while a selection of English cheeses, some nutty, crunchy granary bread, and a bottle of wine will warm the hearts of adults. River pubs, complete with lovely rose gardens, have an appeal for all travelers in nice weather. Lunches are cheaper and more efficient than dinners out for campers on this trip because most of the good campsites are on beaches or moors at some distance from town.

*Based on 1977 rates of exchange.

DAY 1: LONDON/CHICHESTER
(82 miles/131 kilometers)

Proceed south to **Dorking**, via route A24, passing *Box Hill* just to the north. You may be interested in reading for a little taste of the flavor of the area before you go. George Meredith lived on Box Hill, where he wrote *The Egoist*, *The Tragic Comedians*, and *The Adventures of Harry Richmond*. The crucial picnic scene that resolves the action of Jane Austen's *Emma* is set on Box Hill. Dorking is a lovely town located between chalk downs and a sandstone ridge. **Leith Hill**, just south of Dorking, is the highest point in southeastern England. From the tower on top you can see into thirteen counties. *Leith Hill Place* has been in the Wedgewood family for generations and contains a marvelous collection of original jasperware. If you stop at the house in spring or summer, be sure to see and scent the magnificent rhododendron and azalea wood on the grounds.

Continue south on A24 to **Horsham**, an old market town, then on to the south coast. **Worthing** is a resort town, warm and sunny because it is sheltered by the downs, leading to a shingle beach. Turn west on route A259 to **Bognor Regis**, which has a sandy beach. Continue on to **Chichester**, which is laid out in the pattern of a Roman walled town. The walls were built about 200 A.D., and the *City Museum* includes displays of prehistoric, Roman, and medieval periods. *Chichester Cathedral* is Norman in style but has many later additions; the campanile is detached, which is unusual in England. *Goodwood House*, 4 miles from Chichester, is the home of the Duke of Richmond and Gordon; it is three-sided and is noted for its Sussex flintwork. The *Roman Palace*, 1 mile west at **Fishbourne**, was discovered only in 1960 and is especially remarkable for its fine mosaic floor. For sailors, nearby **Bosham** has all types of boats and yachts perched at various angles in the mud at low tide; from mid- to high-tide, the estuary is one of the most active yachting centers on the south coast. Camp in the Chichester area or drive west a few miles to

Fishbourne, Bosham, or **Hayling Island** (which has a number of campgrounds).

ALTERNATE ROUTE

Through **Guildford** on A3 to **Hindhead**, A286 through **Petworth**, and the last leg on A28 to Chichester

DAYS 2 AND 3: CHICHESTER AND THE ISLE OF WIGHT
(20 miles/32 kilometers to ferry)

Portsmouth is 20 miles west of Chichester on A27 and A3. Visitors to the H.M.S. *Victory* (in drydock) will see the spot where Lord Nelson died at the Battle of Trafalgar in 1805. Young seamen, some with elaborate tattoos on their arms, deliver a spirited and interesting account of life on board this well-preserved flagship of one of England's greatest fleets.

After this visit, take a ferry to the **Isle of Wight**, which takes about 30 minutes. The island is 18 miles (north to south) by 22 miles (east to west) and contains a remarkable variety of landscape and many historical sites. Pick a campsite nestled into the cliffs along the rugged southern coast and plan to stay for two nights. (The area called *Undercliff* is especially nice for camping. In addition to Undercliff there are campgrounds at **Sandown**, **Cowes**, and **Ryde**.) There is much to explore by car and by foot. *Carisbrooke Castle*, situated high above the sea near the center of the island, is of Norman origin. King Charles I, his son, and his daughter were all kept prisoner there by Cromwellian forces during the seventeenth century. It is possible to walk completely around the castle on the ramparts if you are not faint of heart while looking down into moats. There is a well house complete with a donkey on a treadmill to bring up heavy buckets. Farther south, *Appuldurcombe House* is a shell of a once magnificent Georgian country house. It belonged to the Worsley family, which once owned most of the island. The curator has interesting stories to tell as you explore the museum, and there is a fascination in wandering through roofless rooms that once were lived in; plaques on the walls indicate the original arrangement. On the north shore near the Solent lies *Osborne House*, built by Queen Victoria, which contains a large collection of furnishings from her era. She used this huge rambling house as a summer residence until her death in 1901. The coastline of the Isle of Wight has many natural beauties such as *The Needles*, three large chalk rocks just offshore rising vertically to 100 feet, and Undercliff, a chalk and limestone plateau which reminds one of the Riviera. Tennyson used to take walks in the woods along this coast near his home, *Farringford House* (to avoid admiring fans). On the other side of the island, **Cowes** is a major sailing center, the home of the Royal Yacht Squadron, which manages Britain's most famous regatta, Cowes Week, each August. The schooner *America* received the cup that bears her name in international yachting competition by winning a race around the Isle of Wight in 1851, with Queen Victoria and Prince Albert watching from the royal yacht. For variety, take the ferry from **Yarmouth**, at the western end of the island, back to the mainland at **Lymington**, which has a harbor packed with boats.

OTHER INTEREST IN THE AREA
Beaulieu Abbey and *Palace House* (14 miles south of South-ampton)

DAYS 4, 5, 6: LYMINGTON/SALCOMBE
(167 miles/267 kilometers)
Some may prefer to poke along this coast, on A337 to **Bournemouth**, A35 to **Poole**, A351 to **Wareham**, A352 to **Dorchester**, A35 to **Lyme Regis**, A3052 to **Exeter** and **Kingsbridge**, and A381 to **Salcombe**. If you want to fully appreciate this section of Dorset you might want to stop for lunch in Lyme Regis, where you can walk the quay John Fowles described in *The French Lieutenant's Woman*. Jane Austen also summered there and set *Persuasion* in Lyme Regis. Others may prefer to proceed west on A337 North to **Cadnam**, left on A31 to **Dorchester**. This is Thomas Hardy country. You may want to read *The Mayor of Casterbridge, Far from the Madding Crowd, The Return of the Native,* or *Tess of the D'Urbervilles*. Then take A35 to **Exeter**, A38 to the exit for **Ugborough** on B3196 to **Kingsbridge**, and A381 to **Salcombe**. This trip will take around five hours, not counting the many stops one is

tempted to make. Allow some time in the Salcombe area to find the perfect campsite for a three-day stay. We found a campground with large flat sites and a view of the sea. The beach was accessible far below. Facilities were among the best we saw anywhere in England. In that area many campsites are bound to be sloping and rocky, which can be difficult with tents. There are also campgrounds in Kingsbridge. You will find small campgrounds all over England, run by families on their fields. In some cases amenities are minimal. Campgrounds are usually spotted by signs on the roads. Salcombe is a very picturesque resort village on the sea in South Devon. Driving is both spectacular and a little terrifying, but worth every minute of it. There are marvelous walks along the high cliffs in the area as well as beaches and boats to ogle and use. *Bolt Head*, a promontory rising steeply out of the sea at the entrance to the estuary, can be reached on foot from Salcombe by a well-marked and well-maintained trail. Farther afield is **Hope Cove**, a charming fishing and resort village that is perfect for a picnic and beach activity.

From Salcombe one can easily make short trips to many other sites in the area. **Plymouth** is an historic seaport especially remembered for the departure of the *Mayflower* in 1620. An elevated promenade overlooking the ocean (called the *Hoe*) provides strollers with a long view of the Sound as far as the *Eddystone Lighthouse*. A statue of Sir Francis Drake stands where he was playing bowls when the news of the sighting of the Armada was brought to him. There is also a gigantic open-air seawater pool with plenty of terraced lounging available. *Dartmoor National Park* is a bleak and desolate wilderness. Tors, granite rocks or caps, rise as much as 2,000 feet into the air, and prehistoric barrows, as well as stone in circles or rows, are scattered about the moor. Hikers should beware of adders, treacherous peat bogs, and mist. It is possible to explore the park by driving back roads, on foot, or on horseback; you will want to leave the main roads to see the wild ponies and enjoy the distinctive flora and fauna of the moor. **Dartmouth** is an old and famous port with the town tumbling down steep hills to the harbor; it is the site of the *Royal Naval College*. **Exeter** is at the center of South Devon and has a number of fine late Georgian houses as well as some medieval architecture. The *Maritime Museum* flanks both sides of the river and has vintage boats of all kinds displayed indoors and out, with the distinction of allowing children (and adults) to climb through them. The Cathedral dates from Norman times and features a geometrically decorated style. Richard Blackmore, who grew up in Exmoor north of Exeter, focused *Lorna Doone* on the area along the coast near the Bristol Channel.

OTHER AREAS OF INTEREST
Penzance (Cornwall)

DAY 7: SALCOMBE/BATH
(125 miles/200 kilometers)

There are three good ways of getting from **Salcombe** to **Bath**. One can either spend some time in the morning exploring **North Devon** (beaches, dunes, or a cliff walk at **Croyde**), via A379 to **Plymouth**, A386 to **Okehampton** and **Bideford**, A39 to **Barnstaple**, A361 to **Braunton**, B3231 to **Croyde** and **Ilfracombe**, A399 to **Blackmore Gate**, B3358 and B3224 through **Exmoor** to **Whedden Cross**, A396 to **Dunster**, A39 to **Bridgewater**, A38 to **Bristol**, and A4 to **Bath.** Alternatively, one can visit *Salisbury Cathedral* driving via **Exeter**, A30 to **Honiton**, A303 and A39 to **Salisbury**. Or one can drive motorways directly to Bath via M5 until it joins M4 at Exit 18, then A46 to Bath. For those who want to loaf, there are virtues in having time to take an unplanned side excursion or arriving early enough to pick out one of the best campsites. Although there are few campgrounds in Bath, there are several in **Cheddar** to the west and one in **Devizes** to the east. There is now an excellent highway from Exeter to Bristol which cuts down driving time if one wishes to do so, but it would be a pity to speed by the beauties of North Devon.

DAY 8: BATH
Bath possesses the only natural hot springs in England. It has been a fashionable watering place since the eighteenth century. Although the old baths are no longer in use and the papers carry

stories about closing the new baths, there is still much for visitors to enjoy. Bath is built of Bath stone, on a series of terraces rising to 600 feet. With baths, churches, parks, and museums available, there is more than enough to fill a day. Many writers focused on the area in and around Bath. You may want to read some of the following before you come: Jane Austen's *Persuasion, Northanger Abbey*; Henry Fielding's *Tom Jones*; Tobias Smollet's *Humphrey Clinker*; Richard Brinsley Sheridan's *The Rival, The School for Scandal*; and Charles Dickens' *Pickwick Papers*.

OTHER AREAS OF INTEREST
Longleat House (4 miles southwest of **Warminster**)

DAY 9: STONEHENGE/AVEBURY CIRCLE
(50 miles/80 kilometers)
Leave Bath on A36 to A303, turn East to A344. **Stonehenge** has fascinated people for ages and continues to puzzle those who are searching for the answers to its design. Guidebooks and scientific papers promote various theories, but no one is quite certain who built Stonehenge or why. Some feel that it was constructed as a temple of worship, possibly to celebrate the winter solstice; others see it as an astronomical observatory. In any case, admiration is due. As you stand by such giant monoliths you cannot help but feel awed by the enormous task of completing such a project. Some of the stones are from only 25 miles away, others from 135 miles away at least; some may have come by sea, others were dragged on rollers. There are also many burial barrows in the area which yield interesting artifacts.

Those who are fascinated by Stonehenge will want to drive on A360 to **Devizes** and A361 to **Avebury**. *Avebury Circle* is the largest stone circle in Britain and probably dates back to the early Bronze Age. It consists of three concentric circles (incomplete in places). The stones are shaped as obelisks. There is also a museum detailing the discovery of a large burial barrow a short distance away.

DAY 10: BATH/OXFORD
(71 miles/114 kilometers)

A route can be planned through the **Cotswolds** on the way to **Oxford**. Picture-postcard villages are dotted through the Cotswold hills. Many of the houses are built of an oolitic stone, contain mullioned windows, and have steep stone roofs. If this kind of scenery is to your taste, take A4 from Bath to Avebury. From Avebury take A361 to **Swindon**, **Lechlade**, and **Burford**, then A424 to **Stow-on-the-Wold**. In nearby **Bourton on the Water** there is a miniature village to delight children as well as adults. Nearby **Moreton-in-Marsh**, **Little Compton**, and **Chipping Norton** also have antique village charm. For those interested in brass rubbing, some of the finest brasses of wool merchants are available in **Northleach**. From the Cotswolds continue east to Oxford on A34 or plan a stop at *Blenheim Palace* on the way. Oxford has few campgrounds, but there is one in **Cassington**, 7 miles west; in **Wallingford**, 12 miles south; and in **Kidlington**, 4 miles north.

Oxford University dates back to the twelfth century as a center of learning. Many of the colleges are built right on High Street and contain traditional quadrangles with chapels, halls, libraries, and gardens. It is delightful to stroll through the gardens at any time of year and enjoy the meticulously kept displays of seasonal flowers. Students and visitors alike enjoy "punting" on the river in flat-bottomed boats that are poled with skill or abandon. College crews compete in various regattas during the year, climaxed in June by Eights Week and the Henley Regatta not far down the Thames. The *Bodleian Library* contains one of the world's most impressive collections of books and manuscripts. The *Ashmolean Museum* houses artifacts from all over the world as well as Britain. Favorite colleges for visitors to stroll through include *Christ Church, St. John's, Magdalen,* and *Trinity.* End your day with an hour or two in a river pub, surrounded by roses and quiet waters. The Trout and The Perch are two among many from which to choose. (*Also see* pages 89–93.)

OTHER INTEREST IN THE AREA

Blenheim Palace (8 miles north of Oxford), seat of the Duke of Wellington and family home of Winston Churchill

DAY 11: OXFORD/LONDON

(57 miles/91 kilometers)

Take M40 for speed, or A423 along the Thames for pleasure through **Wallingford, Henley**, and **Maidenhead**. A stop at Henley can be very pleasant, during racing season or not (*also see* pages 89–93). You can also take A308 to *Windsor Castle*, which is the largest inhabited castle in the world. The State Apartments house many historic treasures, and Queen Mary's doll house will fascinate the whole family. The grounds are pleasant to roam around and you might be lucky enough to watch a changing of the guard (*also see* pages 91–92). Nearby *Eton College* is also worth a visit if you want to catch the flavor of a British "public" school. In London you will find a campground in **Crystal Palace** and one in **Abbey Wood**, both to the southeast.

Summary

This trip can be expanded or condensed. It can take seven days or fourteen days, and you will still not run out of things to do. Without reservations to lock one into a pattern, it is possible to change plans with the weather or as new discoveries appear. This trip has been completed enjoyably by a family with two teenaged children at one time; part of the trip was taken earlier with younger children very successfully. Smaller children are delighted with beaches, boats, miniature villages, ponies, parts of some museums, and small doses of cathedrals. Older children (as well as adults) enjoy in more depth special interests such as maritime history, the different architectural styles found in cathedrals and other historic buildings, art museums, Roman antiquity, prehistoric monoliths, hiking, sailing, and making a personal collection of brass rubbings.

THE CENTRAL CIRCUIT (ENGLAND AND WALES)

From London: Oxford, Stratford, Warwick, Bala, Snowdonia, Lake District, Cambridge
(14 days: 701 miles/1,122 kilometers)

This trip includes a variety of pleasures, beginning with the exploration of the intricate college courtyards in **Oxford**, as long as your feet hold out. A few miles north is a stately home on the grand scale *Blenheim Palace*, the birthplace of Winston Churchill, where you can imagine living in the midst of elegance. Shakespeare country in the **Stratford** area is full of carefully preserved half-timbered houses; a day of exploring Elizabethan memorabilia can be topped by a performance in the *Shakespeare Theatre* (but be sure to order your tickets months in advance). A few miles northeast lie two of England's most interesting castles, *Kenilworth*, in ruins, and *Warwick*, which is very much intact and full of carefully planned displays.

The next section of the trip includes some of the most beautiful, rugged scenery in **Northern Wales** with a great variety of hiking and backpacking available in *Snowdonia National Park*, for both serious climbers and those who prefer gentler walks with gorgeous views. After a brief stop in **Chester**, an ancient and interesting city, you will return to mountains and lakes.

The *Lake District* abounds with winding roads and unexpected views of a distinctive landscape. Shopping is a delight in towns and villages. There are a number of well-marked trails available for hiking, and tourist centers can offer advice for longer treks into the more remote regions.

The return south takes you through or near some of the most interesting cathedral towns of England (**York, Lincoln, Ely**), each worth a half-day stop, on the way to Cambridge. **Cambridge** matches Oxford in many ways but it is more rural at the edges and more compact in the center. As is true of Oxford, Cambridge is best explored on foot. Colleges are scattered all over town, with

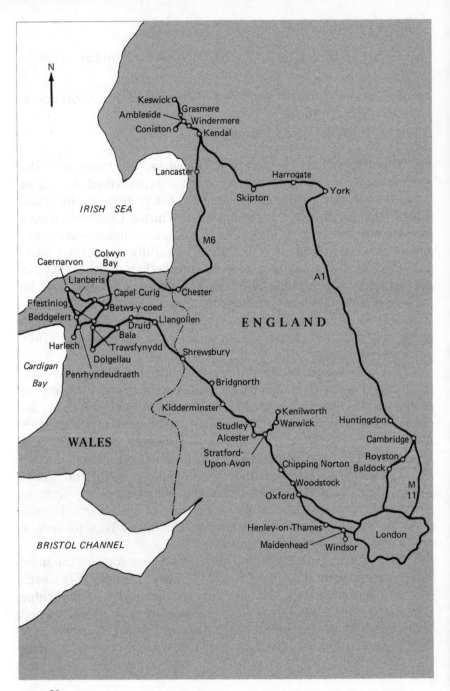

many fronting on the main streets and ending in plowed fields, but they are not far from each other. If your timing is lucky, you might hear the choir as you visit the chapels in *King's College* or *St. John's*. In nice weather it is fun to go "punting on the Cam," which means renting a flat-bottomed boat that is propelled by a pole (not an easy feat). This is one of the best ways to get superb perspective on the large number of colleges lining the banks; students tend to congregate on the banks of the Cam to study, relax, and watch inexpert punters lose their poles and topple into the river. As it began in Oxford, this itinerary ends in Cambridge, with just a short drive taking you back to London.

DAY 1: LONDON/OXFORD
(57 miles/91 kilometers)

Proceed west toward **Oxford** on M40 for speed or M4 for a more leisurely trip. Get off at **Maidenhead** and watch for signs to *Windsor Castle*. Windsor is open all year long and contains a wealth of royal exhibits. (The Queen is in residence when the flag is flying; the State Apartments are open most of the year except for six weeks during the Easter period and three weeks for Ascot.) In the summer Windsor Castle is bound to be crowded and you may have to queue to see the doll house. In the winter, when the guards' uniforms change to a deep purple, they stamp around trying to keep warm, or so our children thought. As students in the fifties, we were fascinated by descriptions of the funeral cortege for King George VI, who had died a few months before, and the coronation of his daughter, then Princess Elizabeth. Most English citizens love and respect the royal family and are deeply interested in their lives. As we noticed during the time Princess Margaret was married, when Queen Elizabeth delivered one of her sons, and again during the Jubilee, each royal family occasion grows into a public pageant. Dedicated Anglophiles will not want to roar by Windsor on the motorway. (*Also see* pages 87–88.)

Windsor Castle itself dates from the twelfth and thirteenth centuries. *St. George's Chapel* has a beautiful collection of stained-glass windows, as well as statues of royal figures, banners, and crests displayed in niches and corners. The doll house, which was given to Queen Mary in 1924, fascinates children and adults alike. From the towers one can catch a glimpse of *Eton College*, one of the most famous English public schools, which is worth a visit if you have time. Shakespeare used *Frogmore*, a country house adjacent to Windsor Great Park, as the setting for *The Merry Wives of Windsor*.

When you leave Windsor, take A423 to **Henley** and wander along the towpath that flanks the Henley Regatta Course, by the various University and rowing clubs that are used by practicing oarsmen much of the year. Henley is a lovely old town to stroll through and has some interesting shops and galleries. It would make a fine luncheon stop. (*Also see* pages 87–88.)

Continue on the A423 to **Oxford**, where you will immediately notice a multitude of spires from churches and colleges. The first stop might be at the tourist information office in the center of town on High Street. There you can collect information on the colleges, maps, theater bookings, and "sound and light" performances (summer outdoor shows based on the history of the area), boating on the Cherwell, museums, and libraries. In addition, you may want to buy one of a series of pamphlets entitled *The Pictorial History of Oxford* published by Pitkin Pictorials, Ltd. here. For those interested in literary history, a great number of writers lived in Oxford while they wrote major works, including Thomas Hobbes, Dr. Samuel Johnson, Percy Bysshe Shelley, Lewis Carroll, Oscar Wilde, Matthew Arnold, Robert Graves, W. H. Auden, Stephen Spender, and J. R. R. Tolkien. Oxford has few campgrounds, but there is one in **Cassington**, 7 miles west; in **Wallingford**, 12 miles south; and in **Kidlington**, 4 miles north. (*Also see* page 88.)

DAY 2: OXFORD/STRATFORD
(33 miles/53 kilometers)

Spend time in the morning touring a limited number of colleges, making sure that you visit the hall, the chapel, and the library (*also see* page 87). There are also several pubs located within remote city courtyards, reached through narrow passageways behind colleges and other buildings where you may enjoy the simple fare and atmosphere of a "pub lunch." There are also a number of pubs located in beautiful settings on rivers near or just at the edge of town. We have enjoyed their gardens in the late afternoon or early evening visiting with friends over a beer while our children played among the rosebushes or fed the fish in the river. (Children are allowed in pub gardens, but not in pubs without a restaurant license.)

Take the A34 to *Blenheim Palace* near **Woodstock** (*also see* page 87). The palace exhibits a fine collection of portraits, tapestries, furniture, and china. The baroque style building was constructed in the early eighteenth century. "Capability" (Lancelot) Brown laid out the gardens, park, and lake. Blenheim is the seat of the Duke of Marlborough, who lives in one wing. Because of its magnitude, proportion, and detail, Blenheim is one of our favorite stately homes in all of England. (You can appreciate these qualities better if you visit Blenheim on a weekday.)

Proceed through **Chipping Norton** to **Stratford-upon-Avon**. We have found campsites on meadows bordering the River Avon to be very convenient and pleasant—in spite of the forward swans. (There are also campgrounds at **Broadway** and **Weir Meadow** in the Vale of Evasham.) Our daughter, when she was 3, extended her hand to a very large swan roaming up from the river and he nipped it, expecting some morsel to eat, then hissed at her for not providing a treat for him. But many English campsites provide such extra inhabitants, whether they be swans, ducks, geese, sheep, or cows. Children love what adults learn to tolerate. You can also rent a boat and go rowing among the swans opposite the *Shakespeare Theatre.*

If you would like to get tickets for the Royal Shakespeare Theatre for the evening you *must* write in advance. The performances are booked ahead for months and sometimes it is impossible to get tickets at all. There is always the chance that a few will be available on the day of the performance, but you cannot count on it. Any that are available can be purchased after 10:30 A.M.; it is often easier to get standing-room tickets, but they are obviously not as comfortable for long performances.

DAY 3: STRATFORD/WARWICK/KENILWORTH/ STRATFORD

(24 miles/38 kilometers)

When we were younger, one highlight of our stay in Stratford was always a walk through the fields out to *Ann Hathaway's Cottage* in the early morning when the dew and mist were still lifting and everything was fresh. Those less romantically inclined can also drive the short distance out there, or take a tour bus. *Shakespeare's Birthplace* and *New Place* are also attractions worth seeing as well as the *Shakespeare Centre*, which opened in the mid 1960s.

When you have satisfied your appetite for Shakespeariana and half-timbered houses, take the A46 for 8 miles to **Warwick** for several hours to tour Warwick Castle. Standing on a steep rock cliff beside the River Avon, this is one of the finest inhabited medieval castles in England. The routes, displays, and descriptions throughout the towers and apartments are beautifully designed to introduce the visitor to medieval life. The castle was fortified over one thousand years ago by Ethelfleda, daughter of King Alfred, complete with dungeons and towers, one of which now houses a fine display of armor. Children particularly enjoy climbing the narrow, circular staircases to the tops of towers where they may imagine themselves in all sorts of heroic roles. The first Lord Brooke turned the inside of the castle into a magnificent residence in the seventeenth century, and it is now the seat of the Earl of Warwick. The State Apartments house a fine collection of paintings by Rubens, Van Dyck, and others.

Capability Brown landscaped the twelve acres of grounds inside and around the castle walls, and it shows in varied elevations, sudden vistas, and a mixture of formal gardens and rural parkland. Once we were lucky enough to happen upon a group of Morris dancers on the grounds. These are men who dress in traditional costume and dance, usually to celebrate the harvest. Their dancing is full of knee slapping, whoops, and hollers which appeal greatly to children. The gardens are inhabited not only by live peacocks but also by a collection of sculptured peacocks in the hedges. Once we were treated to the mating dance of a peacock who tried in vain to interest a female; she showed utter disdain for him no matter how widely he fanned his beautiful turquoise feathers.

From Warwick it is only a little over 4 miles to **Kenilworth** on the A46. Henry I gave Kenilworth to his chamberlain, Geoffrey de Clinton, in 1122. The Keep, which is the first masonry building in England, was built between 1150 and 1175. In 1362 John of Gaunt added the Banquet Hall, the White Hall, and the Strong Tower. Elaborate entertaining went on over the centuries in this magnificent castle until it fell into ruin. Do read *Kenilworth* by Sir Walter Scott before you go.

DAY 4: STRATFORD/BALA
(108 miles/173 kilometers)

Take A422 to **Alcester**, A435 to **Studley**, A448 to **Bromsgrove** through **Kidderminster**, A442 to **Bridgnorth**, and A458 to **Shrewsbury**. Shrewsbury, the county town of Shropshire, is full of lovely Tudor buildings. It makes a nice lunch stop with plenty of interesting things to see. To get a sense of what rural life once was like in this hilly corner of England, you may want to read *A Shropshire Lad* by A. E. Housman before your trip.

Continue on the A5 into Wales through **Llangollen** to **Druid** and then take the A494 to **Bala**, which is set in rolling hills leading down to the largest natural lake and one of the finest sailing centers in Wales. (Bala has fascinated us because our ancestors left a farm on the hillside there in 1698 to settle in Bala Cynwd, Pennsylvania when persecution of Quakers drove them out of this beautiful land.) Look for a campsite near the lake or up on the hill on the road (B440) leading to **Llandrillo.** In town, the shopping district (look for Welsh tapestry woolens) is several blocks long, and it is pleasant to stroll the length of it without meeting the crowds of some resort towns. Once in October we were lucky enough to be there during a fair; vendors brought Welsh crafts from all parts of Wales, so we almost completed our Christmas shopping. The main business of the fair was a day-long auction of Welsh black cattle and sheep, attended by men dressed in sport coats and ties, mostly in sombre earth colors, and there were also rides and food stalls which delighted our children.

DAY 5: BALA/SNOWDONIA
(31 miles/50 kilometers)

Bala is one natural gateway to the *Snowdonia National Park*. Driving in that direction is breathtakingly beautiful with rugged scenery on all sides. From Bala take the A494 to **Dolgellau** (where you will find more wool shops) and the A470 to **Ffestiniog**. A lonely but spectacular alternate route is the A4212 over the high moors (be sure to close the sheep gates) to **Trawsfynydd** and the A470 to **Ffestiniog**. Then take the A487 to **Penrhyndeudraeth**. At this point you may want to take a short side trip south on the A496 to *Harlech Castle*, one of the most rugged in a series of castles built by Edward I. Though once directly on the sea, it now lies half a mile inland with sand flats below, yet still perches over all the countryside with commanding views on all sides. After returning to Penrhyndeudraeth, take the A4085 to **Beddgelert**, where you may want to camp in the state park or in nearby private campsites. For alternative bases in Snowdonia, you may choose to take a scenic mountain road that skirts the east flank of the mountain for 8 more miles northeast until you reach the A4086. If you turn left toward **Llanberis** you will find a number of campsites that are very primitive in alpine meadows (mountain tents are advised). If you prefer more amenities, turn right onto the A4086, through **Capel Curig**, and continue on the A5 to **Betws-y-Coed**, a beautiful and comfortable resort town 17 miles from Beddgelert. Welsh woolen and craft shops abound here.

DAYS 6, 7: SNOWDONIA

For serious mountaineering, get contour maps that are available for planning trips. For less strenuous hiking and walking, drive to the height of the pass on A4086 towards **Llanberis** and walk in to **Llydaw**, near the center of the group of peaks making up Mount Snowdon. There is a lovely lake there, and the walk is not difficult. In Llanberis there is a railway that climbs to the top of the mountain complex.

You can also take a trip to *Caernarvon Castle* by continuing on through Llanberis. Set where the river joins the sea, it is considered the most important of Edward I's castles, and Prince Charles' Investiture was here in 1969. The outer walls are 8 to 14 feet thick and you can climb up into many towers and look over the ramparts, continuing along the perimeter on walkways between them. (Some views downward might not appeal to the faint-hearted.) This castle really looks like the castles we imagine as children, with dark winding staircases, small, damp stone chambers with a single window looking out beyond the castle walls, and plenty of secret passageways. There are also some very fine exhibits on the castle's role in history, including displays on the recent Investiture.

DAY 8: BETWS-Y-COED/WINDERMERE
(157 miles/251 kilometers)

Take the A470 north to **Colwyn Bay**, the A55 to **Chester**, which is a fascinating old town and would make a good lunch stop. You may enjoy a walk around the walls that follow the line of the Roman city walls and also include the castle. Chester is one of the most medieval-looking cities in England. The timbered houses are beautifully preserved. Take the A56 to **Hapsford**, the M56 east and the M6 north (possibly getting off at **Lancaster** for a side excursion to the cathedral and town rich in the history of the War of the Roses). Continue on the M6 until exit 36, take the A65 to **Kendal** and the A591 to **Windermere**.

Windermere, a town on the largest lake in England and an old resort and touring center, is a good spot to begin exploring this famous corner of England. The Lake District is a national park that lies within the boundaries of the three northern counties of Westmorland, Cumberland, and Lancashire. The terrain here is full of contrast between high mountains and deep lakes. The many lakes, lined with woods and overshadowed by craggy rocks, are interspersed with green valleys containing gentle streams and lush pastures. *Scafell Pike* is the highest peak in England at 3,210 feet. The terrain for hiking in this area (the *Langdale Pikes*) is more rugged and barren but leads to spectacular views. Boats may be rented on the lakes, pony trekking is a popular way to see the more remote regions, and good fishing is available in both lakes and rivers. For those interested in literary history, the area abounds with artifacts and memorabilia of William Wordsworth (**Rydal** and **Grasmere**), Samuel Taylor Coleridge (**Keswick**), John Ruskin (**Coniston**), Hugh Walpole, Arthur Ransome, Gilbert Scott, Matthew Arnold, William Edward Forster, John Keats, Percy Bysshe Shelley, Thomas Carlyle, Alfred Lord Tennyson, and Beatrix Potter. There are many local crafts available in the district, some found in the workshops where they are made. Look especially for sweaters, scarves, woven shawls, and blankets.

Camping areas are often primitive but beautiful. Check your camping guide, and get as much information as you can from the tourist offices in towns. We have enjoyed camping at *Grasmere* in a sloping meadow on the northwest side of the lake with village and mountain before us. There are more rugged campsites in the *Langdale Pikes* and some with more amenities at **Keswick** on *Derwent Water* and on *Lake Windermere*. Our favorite was the area near the head of *Lake Coniston*, situated just below the Old Man of Coniston peak and across the lake from John Ruskin's house. There were no amenities except toilets and sinks in one part of an old ruin, and we discovered that the lights were turned off at 8:30 P.M., just as we were approaching, toothbrushes in hand. We shared a grassy meadow with sheep and cows (and a few bulls, which kicked over our very hastily vacated camp chairs), and we were mesmerized by the conjunction of mountain and calm water in one of the most idyllic views possible. This campground, located just east of the village of **Coniston**, is not listed in any of the guide books but we we had heard about it from campers the night before.

DAYS 9, 10, 11: LAKE DISTRICT

Here you must make choices. There is more than enough to keep you enjoying your days and wishing you had more time to explore this extraordinary landscape. Suggestions include visiting any of the museums and homes lived in by literary figures, climbing in the *Langdale Pikes* region, hiking in the **Grasmere** area, climbing the *Old Man of Coniston*, taking the National Trust walk on the ridge near *Ullswater* (including *Glencoyne Park* and a hike up *Airaforce*), taking boat trips on the lakes, shopping Keswick, Grasmere, Windermere and other villages, driving the tortuous but rewarding roads over *Wyrnose Pass, Styhead Pass, Knott Pass,* or *Eskdale Pass.* Favorite areas for serious climbers include *Wasdale Head, Great Langdale, Borrowdale, Ennerdale, Coniston, Great Gable, Pillar Rock, Dow Crag,* and *Scafell.* (Note: The Lake District gets a great deal of rain, but wet weather need not hinder the enjoyment of campers who come prepared with good, light waterproofs—both jackets and trousers—and, above all, Wellingtons or a pair of similar heavy rubber boots.)

DAY 12: WINDERMERE/CAMBRIDGE
(247 miles/395 kilometers)

When you have done all you can in the Lake District, take the A591 to **Kendal**, the A65 to **Skipton**, the A59 through **Harrogate** to **York** for a lunch stop. The cathedral here is the largest medieval church in England and there is also a castle, as well as several museums. (You may wish to linger and add an extra day to the itinerary.) Then take the A64 toward **Leeds**, meet the A1 at **Thorne**, and continue south to **Huntingdon**, where you will take the A604 to **Cambridge**. Alternatively, if your family has developed a strong interest in cathedrals, take the extra time to leave the A1 via the A57 and visit **Lincoln**, or leave at **Huntingdon** via the A1123 until it joins the A10, turning north for **Ely**. (If you do this, do not plan to reach Cambridge in one day from Windermere). Camp in one of the many pleasant villages surrounding Cambridge where there are grounds, such as **Comberton, Coton,** or **Trumpington**; there is no camping in the city itself. There is a campground east of **Huntingdon** (which is northwest of Cambridge) and one southwest of **Newmarket** (which is northeast of Cambridge); there is no camping in the city itself.

DAY 13: CAMBRIDGE

We lived in Cambridge for ten months and have a special fondness for the city. Cambridge began life as a Roman camp and grew through commerce by road and river; it became the market town for much of the region between London and East Anglia. In 1068 a castle was built as the center of royal power in the region. In 1209, when scholars in Oxford had to leave following trouble with the townspeople, some came to Cambridge and slowly developed a sister university by founding colleges, beginning with *Peterhouse* in 1284. There are now twenty-three separate colleges affiliated with the University, each with its own Master, Fellows, and Scholars. All the colleges are built around courtyards, bright with flowers in season; all have chapels, halls (for dining), common rooms, and libraries. The University consists of a ruling body, the Regent House, composed of all office-holders in the University and the Colleges. The Council of the Senate includes four heads of Colleges, four Professors, and eight members of Regent House. The University sets examinations and awards degrees; the colleges prepare students through tutorials and provide a congenial residence for them. Most of the students live in their colleges and study a single subject for three years. In addition, they may take advantage of the rich cultural life available in Cambridge.

Among the many special things one can choose to do in Cambridge, we suggest this college tour: park on the "backs" (the backs of the colleges as opposed to the front entrances on one of the city streets) on Queens Road or on Silver Street. Walk through the old sections of *Queens College*, where in June you may be lucky enough to attend a Shakespearean performance against the backdrop of the lovely old half-timbered buildings dating from the sixteenth century, and red brick from 1448. This is one of the most interesting grouping of old college buildings in Cambridge. Walk across the street into *Corpus Christi College*, which was founded in 1352. There is a memorial tablet in the old courtyard for Christopher Marlowe, who was a student there in the sixteenth century. Continue along King's Parade to *King's College*, founded in 1441 by Henry VI; it has a magnificent chapel walled with glorious windows, built with the help of Henry VIII. They were created by English and Flemish craftsmen and portray scenes from both the New Testament and the Old Testament. The carved screen was added in 1533 and contains the initials of Henry VIII and Anne Boleyn. At the far end stands the *Adoration of the Magi* by Rubens. You may have heard the King's College Choir during a Christmas service on radio or television. On December 24 we walked by a long line of people who had been waiting since the previous afternoon to get a seat inside for the Christmas concert; they had provided themselves with sleeping bags, blankets, lawn chairs, food, and wine for the long wait. *Clare College* is next with an old courtyard in perfect proportions and beautiful gardens stretching down to the river. After leaving Clare, walk north on Trinity Lane to Senate House Passage and dip into *Gonville and Caius* (pronounced 'Keys') *College* to see the clock tower. Head back through the college to Trinity Street and enter the main gate of *Trinity College*, which was founded by Henry VIII in 1546 and is the largest college in the University. There is an ornate fountain in the center of the Great Court, and a clock tower (also known as the Edward III Gate). Christopher Wren designed the library, which was built in 1676; it contains many valuable books and manuscripts, which may be seen between the hours of 1 and 4 P.M. on weekdays. Trinity Street then becomes St. John's Street, where you may walk into *St. John's College*, continuing through its many courtyards, each in a different architectural style, over the imitation of Venice's Bridge of Sighs (with its barred windows to keep undergraduates in), and into the New Court and out onto Magdalene Street (see the row of sixteenth- and seventeenth-century houses in this section). Across the street is *Magdalene College*, founded in 1428 as a home for Benedictine monks from abbeys in the region who were studying in Cambridge. The library of Samuel Pepys is located there. When you leave Magdalene, walk back down Bridge Street to St. John's Street, Trinity Street, and King's Parade to *St. Mary's Church*, where you can climb the tower and look over all the colleges you have been through. You may want to replenish your fresh fruits, vegetables, cheeses, or almost anything else you need in the open market located next to the church before heading down King's Parade to your car.

This is but a small sample of Cambridge. For those who can stay longer there are many activities ranging from "rubbing" the brass of Roger de Trumpington—the second oldest and one of the best-preserved brasses in England—in the nearby village of **Trumpington** to visiting country houses and cathedrals in the surrounding area. To the north we especially enjoyed visiting *Burghley House*, a sixteenth-century mansion built by Elizabeth I's Lord High Treasurer, William Cecil, and loaded with art treasures (located near **Stamford**); the cathedral in **Peterborough** where both Katherine of Aragon and Mary, Queen of Scots, are buried; and the beautifully proportioned cathedral in **Ely**, which dates from the twelfth century and dominates the countryside for miles around. To the southeast *Audley End Mansion*, near **Saffron Walden,** is a lovely Jacobean country house dating from 1603. Also to the southeast are the charming medieval wool towns of **Cavendish** and **Lavenham**, which are filled with picturesque half-timbered buildings leaning at all angles. To the south is *Hatfield House*, another Jacobean house built in 1611 to replace an older home in which Elizabeth I grew up. To the west is *Woburn Abbey,* an eighteenth-century mansion containing various fine art and china collections but unfortunately a little overdone by the addition of "tourist" attractions (go off-season).

DAY 14: CAMBRIDGE/LONDON
(60 miles/96 kilometers)

Return to **London** by the A130 to the A11 and M11 for the *City* (financial district), or take the A10 to **Royston,** the A505 by **Baldock,** the A1 (M) and the A1 for the *West End* (theaters and shopping).

SUMMARY

This trip can also be expanded or condensed, and you can plan time in London before the trip begins or afterward. We enjoyed this trip with teenaged children once, and part of it again with relatives up to the age of 90. We felt that 14 days were not enough to linger very long anywhere, but it was possible to follow the itinerary without feeling rushed. Some travelers may choose to spend more time in Oxford or Cambridge; climbers or hikers might prefer a longer stay in Snowdonia. We have spent time in the Lake District on three separate trips, mostly in soggy weather, but that choice would not appeal to everyone.

SCOTLAND

From Edinburgh: St. Andrews, Aberdeen, Balmoral Castle, Pitlochry, Inverness, Isle of Skye, Fort William, Oban, Stirling, Edinburgh
(14 days: 676 miles/1,082 kilometers)

Caledonia, as Scotland was called long ago, was inhabited by the Picts (who lived north of the Firth of Forth and Clyde) and the Celts (who occupied the land south into England) until the Roman invasion in 82 A.D. The enmity dating from those ancient times has continued through the ages as southerners sought to grasp Scotland. Although the Romans left in 410 A.D., Scotland battled with Norsemen as well as their English neighbors, finally declaring war on England in 1542. In 1603 the accession of James VI of Scotland to the throne of England as James I signified the first union of Scotland and England. A series of rebellions, invasions, and murders followed, including the attempt of Bonnie Prince Charlie to take over the throne in 1746. The spirit of the Scots continues to be strong (as evidenced by the home rule controversy in recent years), and although Scotland and England cooperate, the Scots take great pride in Caledonian traditions and history.

Visitors to Scotland often become intrigued by the legends and the romance as they walk through the haunts of Mary, Queen of Scots, Bonnie Prince Charlie, Sir Walter Scott, or Robert Burns. The traditions of the clans, with their colorful kilts and Highland dances, fascinate; the haunting music of bagpipes, perhaps heard on a clear starlit night at the *Tattoo* in front of *Edinburgh Castle*, stays with you forever.

The land itself includes a surprising variety of contour and color ranging from green glens, purple heather on moors and heaths, brown bogs and flatlands, craggy rocks on mountains, and blue alpine lakes and fjords. The natural features of this beautiful country lend themselves to sports enthusiasts. You can fish for trout and salmon, play golf on the famous *St. Andrews* course, ski

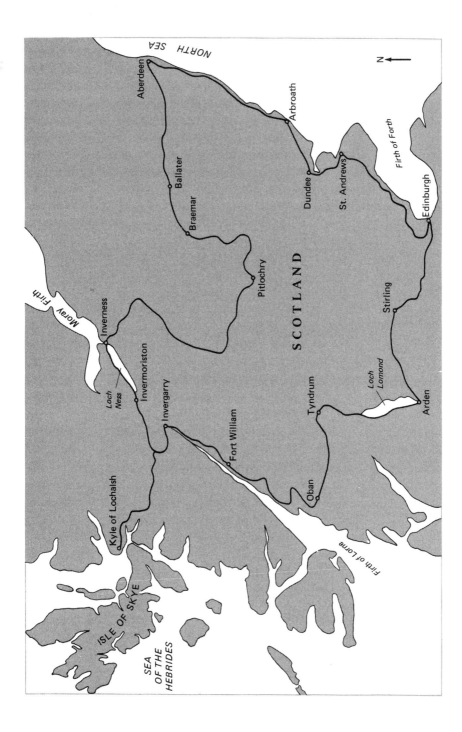

in the *Cairngorm* area, sail on the lakes, climb and go pony trekking in the *Highlands*. Much of Scotland is rugged, wild, and lonely, appealing to those who seek solitude rather than crowds and cafes.

This trip begins with a day in Edinburgh. (You may want to add another day there, or perhaps part of a day at the end of the trip.) A drive up the coast stopping in **St. Andrews** and some of the little fishing villages on the way leads you to **Aberdeen**. There are a number of castles to visit between Aberdeen and **Pitlochry**, as well as the church the Royal Family attends in **Crathie**, near **Balmoral**. Pitlochry, **Braemar**, or **Aviemore** can be jumping-off places for climbing in the Highlands. **Inverness** is steeped in history and is also a convenient base for a day trip along the coast or the shores of Loch Ness, where you may hope to see the monster. To the west, the **Isle of Skye** is the largest and most romantic of the *Inner Hebrides*. The *Cuillins* are mountains that attract experienced climbers, *Dunvegan Castle* reminds one of the original purpose of castles, and the rugged terrain of the island opens up startling prospects for those who can appreciate the beauties of barren land. Back on the mainland, *Ben Nevis*, the tallest mountain in the British Isles, overlooks the town of **Fort William**. Continuing along the coast to **Oban**, you can pause to enjoy the pleasures of this resort area, then dip inland to enjoy the lush shores of *Loch Lomond*. Finally, *Stirling Castle* reminds you of the embattled history of Scotland.

DAY 1: EDINBURGH

The center of **Edinburgh** is Princes Street, which is approximately 1 mile long and runs from east to west. On the north side are shops of all kinds, many of which sell tartans, bagpipes, and other symbols of Scottish tradition, as well as beautiful woolen sweaters and blankets. The views from the street are extraordinary, especially the panorama of the over-hanging castle and the intricacies of the *Old Town*, seen from the Princes Street Gardens in the foreground. People have lived on this ridge, which runs from *Castle Rock* to *Holyrood Palace*, for many centuries. When the street and surrounding Old Town could hold no more inhabitants, the *New Town* was developed. The *Mound* was made with earth dug from the foundations of the New Town and now separates East and West Princes Street Gardens. The *Castle*, occupied by both Scottish and English forces at various times, dates from the eleventh century. If you are there in late August or early September during the Edinburgh Festival, you can enjoy the famous *Tattoo*. We have enjoyed this thrilling performance on a cold, crisp, clear starlit night, shivering from the cold but moved by watching Scotsmen, dancing and marching to bagpipe music with kilts swirling. The music is haunting and the pride and honor of a country are evident in the performance. While touring the Castle during the day, you may walk through the *Royal Apartments*, the museum of armor, and see the *Scottish Regalia* or *Honors of Scotland* in the *Crown Chamber*. Near the Chapel is *Mons Meg*, a fifteenth-century cannon and a newer 25-pound howitzer which fires over the city at one o'clock each day. *St. Margaret's Chapel* itself was built in 1076 by the daughter-in-law of King Duncan, whose murder is the source of conflict in *Macbeth*.

Continue down the *Royal Mile*, dipping into the *High Kirk of St. Giles*, which is the principal church of Edinburgh. The *Chapel of the Thistle* has beautiful stained-glass heraldic windows and elaborately carved stalls. Then you will pass *Parliament House*, the *City Chambers*, *John Knox's House*, built in the sixteenth century, and *Canongate Tolbooth*, once a jail and now a museum. At the end of the street you will find *Holyrood Palace*, which is the official residence of the Queen when she is in Scotland. The palace was originally a guest house for the abbey in the twelfth century, and Bonnie Prince Charlie lived there in 1745 during his attempt to seize the castle and win the crown. Mary, Queen of Scots, lived there from 1561 to 1567; in her apartments there is a brass tablet which marks the spot where her alleged lover, David Rizzio, was murdered by her husband Lord Darnley and other nobles. Nearby are the ruins of *Holyrood Abbey*, which was built by King David I, as one legend goes, in gratitude for his deliverance from the attack of a wild stag by the appearance of a Holy Cross or Rood. Others say that the abbey was named after the True Cross belonging to St. Margaret, his mother. The *King's Park*, located southeast of the palace, contains *Arthur's Seat*, an 823-foot chunk of volcanic rock that provides an excellent view of Edinburgh.

Those who would like to follow a literary tour can visit *Lady Stair's House*, which has a collection of the memorabilia of Robert Burns, Robert Louis Stevenson, and Sir Walter Scott. The Robert Louis Stevenson house is at 8 Howard Place; Sir Walter Scott's is at 39 Castle Street.

There is a large campground in north Edinburgh that is fully equipped with facilities. There are also campgrounds located in **Kinross, Kirkcaldy, Kinghorn, Comrie, Newbridge,** and **Haddington.**

DAY 2: EDINBURGH/ABERDEEN
(133 miles/213 kilometers)

Cross the graceful, much-photographed *Firth of Forth Bridge* on A90, take A92 to **Kirkcaldy,** and A915 to **St. Andrews,** the site of the oldest university in Scotland (started in 1412), a ruined cathedral, castle, and a number of medieval churches as well as the famed golf course. (Golfers may want to spend more time here.) Next take the A91 and A919, then A92 to **Dundee,** which was known in the eighteenth century as a whaling port, and for its marmalade, then as the center of the jute industry in the nineteenth century. Continue on A92 to **Arbroath,** a pleasant fishing port containing the ruins of a twelfth-century cathedral. *Dunnottar Castle,* a fourteenth-century fortress, is almost completely surrounded by the sea just south of **Stonehaven.** Continue on the A92 to **Aberdeen** where there is a 2-mile-long beach, a thriving fishing industry, a leading university, and some grim relics of the past like the tolbooth and the guillotine. Aberdeen is also within easy range of a large number of castles located between the coast and the Grampian Mountains.

There is a campground in the city, plus one at **Nigg** (2 miles away), **Skene** (10 miles west), and at **Inverbervie** (south of Aberdeen). There are many campgrounds north of Aberdeen in **Fraserburgh** and **Peterhead.** Most of these are on the sea, with beaches, but campgrounds listing a beach do not guarantee that they are suitable for swimming.

DAY 3: ABERDEEN/PITLOCHRY
(105 miles/168 kilometers)

Take A93 along the River Dee into the Eastern Highlands. Fourteen miles west of Aberdeen is *Crathes Castle*. Then **Ballater,** near *Balmoral Castle,* the residence of the Royal Family, which is not open to the public but can be glimpsed from the road on a curve of the River Dee. *Crathie Church,* where the Royal Family attends services while in residence, is nearby. As students we waited for hours to see the Queen there on a beautiful Sunday morning in late August. We went into the church early in the morning and found it peaceful and rich with the colors of the stained-glass windows and the velvet on the pews and kneeling cushions. Back along the road leading up to the church we decided on a spot for waiting, along with the other people who had gathered there. At 11:30 the royal procession began moving up the hill to the church. First came a bagpipe followed by the Black Watch Guard, next, in cars, the Duke of Gloucester and the Duke of Kent and the royal staff, and another car bearing Princess Margaret and the Queen Mother, and at the end another with Queen Elizabeth and Prince Phillip. A nearly perfect morning closed with a walk up the hill to get a view of Balmoral Castle, nestled in a stand of pine near the river.

Continue on A93 to **Braemar,** the site of the Highland Games in September, continue to the *Bridge of Cally,* then take A924 to **Pitlochry.** This is a very popular resort area and there are a number of campgrounds in Pitlochry as well as in **Kenmore, Aberfeldy, Dunkeld,** and **Blair Atholl.**

ALTERNATE ROUTE

Hikers who want to climb the Cairngorms may prefer to camp near Braemar or continue on the A9 to **Aviemore** (on the way to **Inverness**). A chairlift located near Aviemore runs both winter and summer. Aviemore may well be the ideal location to camp for a day or two. The problem is covering the distance from Aberdeen in one day over mountain passes. You may want to stay longer in Braemar and then drive to Aviemore in one day.

DAY 4: PITLOCHRY
(OR BRAEMAR OR AVIEMORE)

Any of these towns may be used as a base for pleasant hikes.

DAY 5: PITLOCHRY/INVERNESS
(85 miles/136 kilometers)

Take the A9 to **Inverness**. Macbeth's castle once stood in the center of Inverness; the city is now the leading shopping and tourist center of the area.

DAY 6: INVERNESS AND AREA

In **Inverness**, the capital of the Highlands, traditional Highland dancers perform throughout the summer, and there are special Highland Games in July. You can enjoy the multiplying legends and fanfare about the *Loch Ness Monster*, which has been sighted for hundreds of years. The site of the *Battle of Culloden*, where Bonnie Prince Charlie was defeated by the Duke of Cumberland in 1746, is marked by a tall cairn (rock) and scattered headstones. East of Inverness you may drive along the coast of the Moray Firth. Resorts such as **Nairn, Elgin, Findhorn,** and **Lossiemouth** offer wide beaches and various sports such as golf and sailing. Boats for longer cruises on Loch Ness and the rest of the Caledonian Canal are available. The Inverness area contains several campgrounds. There is one in **Beauly** that is 12 miles west and one in **Kessock** on the shore that is accessible by car ferry.

DAY 7: INVERNESS/ISLE OF SKYE
(82 miles/131 kilometers)

Take A82 along beautiful Loch Ness to **Invermoriston**, A887 and A87 to the ferry at **Kyle of Lochalsh** for the Isle of Skye. On the way you will pass *Eileen Donan Castle* in **Dornie**, set beautifully on an islet connected to the mainland by a narrow causeway. We have camped without benefit of a campground on the Isle of Skye for one night. There is a campground at **Broadford** that has a beach.

ALTERNATE ROUTE

Those who have days to spare and the desire to explore one of the most rugged seacoasts in the world may wish to circle north on A9 and A838 to the *Pentland Firth*, which separates the mainland and the **Orkney Islands**. The seas encountered between *Duncansby Head* and *Cape Wrath* are reputed to be among the wildest in the oceanic world.

DAY 8: ISLE OF SKYE

Portree, a town with a sheltered harbor, is the capital of the Isle of Skye. It is a good center for touring, as are **Broadford** and **Sligachan**. The island is beautiful, wild, lonely, and quite primitive. The *Cuillins* are the most memorable mountains in Britain; the pinnacles are precipitous and often shrouded in mist. Most of the climbs will appeal only to experienced climbers. John MacLeod, the present clan chief, occupies *Dunvegan Castle* for several months each year with his family. At one time the castle was only accessible by the sea through a small gateway with an opening on the rocks; there is now a bridge across a ravine which was originally a moat. Among the objects preserved in the castle you can see the *Fairy Flag*, which has twice saved the clan on the battlefield. Flora Macdonald is a name well known to all Skye residents. In 1746 she disguised Prince Charles as her maid, Betty Burke, and rowed him to Skye to hide from Royal Forces.

DAY 9: ISLE OF SKYE/FORT WILLIAM
(73 miles/117 kilometers)

Take A87 to **Invergarry**, A82 to **Fort William**. Highland Games are held here in August and there is a West Highland Museum to visit. The most striking feature of this area is *Ben Nevis*, the tallest mountain in The British Isles (4,406 feet). This mountain, a towering granite mass, does not show a cone or peak. *Glen Nevis* is one of the finest glens in Scotland, ascending the left bank of the Nevis and passing the site of a medieval fort, a waterfall, and a spectacular gorge.

Spean Bridge, northeast of Fort William, has a number of campgrounds. There is one in Fort William, a short distance toward Glen Nevis along A82. Others may be found in **Ballachulish, Glencoe, Kinlochleven,** and **Archaracis.**

DAY 10: FORT WILLIAM AND BEN NEVIS

Climbers may want to reach the top of Ben Nevis; some have suggested that it usually takes four hours to climb up and three to come down. Experienced climbers may try the hazardous north faces; others may enjoy the 5-mile trail that begins on the bank of the River Nevis. You may wish to visit *Glencoe* ("glen of weeping" in Gaelic), the scene of a massacre in 1692. Apparently MacDonald of Glencoe had refused to take the oath of allegiance to the king until the very last minute, and then when he tried to do so found no magistrate available in Fort William and had to travel to Inverary. When the papers finally arrived in Edinburgh they were hidden and the clan was eliminated. Cambell of Glenlyon and 128 soldiers attacked the inhabitants at dawn, killing more than 40 of 200.

DAY 11: FORT WILLIAM/OBAN
(64 miles/102 kilometers)

Take A82 and A828 to Oban. Campgrounds with beaches may be found at **Scammadale,** 13 miles south; and at **Benderloch,** 10 miles north of Oban.

DAY 12: OBAN AND ISLANDS

Oban is a resort area enjoyed by yachtsmen, fishermen, and other vacationers. Steamers carry visitors to islands in the Inner Hebrides such as *Mull* and *Staffa.* An uninhabited island, Staffa was once the scene of a volcanic action in which liquid basalt was spewed to the surface. The cooling and coagulating of these masses produced a series of curious rock columns. *Fingal's Cave,* which looks like a cathedral of rock, is 227 feet long, and the depth of the water at mid-tide is 66 feet. It is possible to go in by boat. *Mull,* "a mass of hill," has cliffs, beaches, lakes, and a network of sealochs and creeks on the west side that remind one of an archipelago. In 1588 the *Florencia,* a galleon of the Spanish Armada, was blown up and sunk in the harbor of **Tobermory.** Since the seventeenth century, divers have explored the hulk searching for treasure.

DAY 13: OBAN/STIRLING
(102 miles/163 kilometers)

Take A85 to **Tyndrum**, A82 to **Arden** along the beautiful shores of Loch Lomond, where you may want to stop for a picnic or swim. Then take A811 to **Stirling.** There are several campgrounds in or near Stirling; two have beaches. Stirling lies in the center of Scotland and has played an important part in its history; it is situated between two famous battlefields. Southeast of Stirling is **Bannockburn**, where Robert the Bruce defeated King Edward's army in 1314. To the northeast, on *Abbey Craig,* is a tower marking the site where Sir William Wallace defeated an English army in 1297. *Stirling Castle* stands on a precipitous cliff overlooking the town. Alexander I died in the castle in 1124 and William the Lion in 1214; four of Scotland's six Jameses lived here, including James VI, the son of Mary, Queen of Scots, who spent his boyhood here. During the reign of the Stuarts, James I of England turned the castle into a luxurious residence. Nearby *Doune Castle,* a restored fortress from the fifteenth century, was built by Robert, Duke of Albany, and his son, Murdoch. When Murdoch was executed in 1425 the Crown seized the castle. In 1745 the hero of Scott's *Waverley* was detained there.

DAY 14: STIRLING/EDINBURGH
(32 miles/51 kilometers)
Take A9 and M9 to **Edinburgh**.

Summary

Scotland has enough beauty and serenity to entice travelers to linger. There are many spots which will appeal to people for longer stays. However, it would be difficult to compress this trip easily because driving can be slow. For travelers with very limited time we suggest omitting an entire area such as the trip to Aberdeen, Inverness, the Isle of Skye, or Oban.

SCANDINAVIA

From Copenhagen: Helsingør, Öland, Stockholm, Ölslo, Sogne-
fjord, Jostedal Glacier, Hardangerfjord, Bergen, Stavanger, Kris-
tiansand, Århus, Odense, Copenhagen
(24 days: 1,590 miles/2,544 kilometers)

Scandinavia is made up of five countries, each with a different though related language and varied topography, but with a common history of alternating strife and cooperation. The countries have developed alongside one another, exchanged pieces of land and sometimes kings, fought and negotiated peace, traded with one another—all while maintaining independence and yet sharing many common elements in a recognizable culture. Norway and Sweden are contained in a large peninsula extending to the North Cape and separating the Baltic from the Atlantic. Finland meets the base of this peninsula and lies a short distance across the Baltic from Sweden, which has encouraged interaction through trade. Denmark, although completely separate geographically on another peninsula and a series of islands, was linked to Sweden in earlier times when part of the peninsula belonged to Denmark. Remote and isolated Iceland once belonged to Denmark, and shares its culture. (Those who are particularly interested in Scandinavia may want to make one transatlantic crossing via Icelandic Airlines with a layover for several days or a week to explore its magnificent landscape.) In 1953 Norway, Sweden, Denmark, and Iceland formed a Nordic Union which Finland later joined.

The topography of Scandinavia was shaped during the Ice Age by giant glaciers which chiseled their way down valleys to the ocean, leaving fjords and islands. All of northern Scandinavia was covered with ice until 10,000 years ago. This heavy ice caused the land to sink and then rise again when the ice melted. The land is still rising, perhaps 15 inches in each century, which necessitates changes in harbor use and facilities.

Human beings entered Scandinavia between 10,000 and 5,000

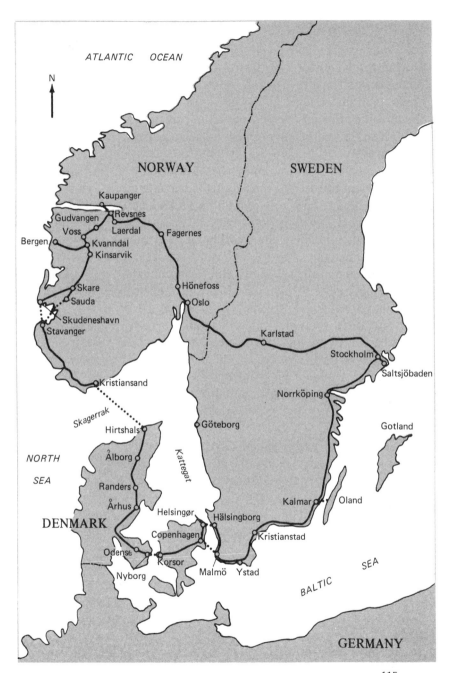

ATLANTIC OCEAN

N

NORWAY   SWEDEN

Kaupanger
Revsnes
Gudvangen
Voss   Laerdal   Fagernes
Bergen
Kvanndal
Kinsarvik

Skare   Hönefoss
Sauda   Oslo
Skudeneshavn
Stavanger   Karlstad

Stockholm
Saltsjöbaden

Kristiansand
Norrköping

Skagerrak
Hirtshals   Göteborg   Gotland

NORTH
SEA   Ålborg

Kattegat

Randers

Århus   Kalmar   Oland
Helsingør   Hälsingborg
DENMARK   Copenhagen   Kristianstad
Odense   Korsor
Nyborg   Malmö   Ystad   SEA

BALTIC

GERMANY

B.C., during the Epipalaeolithic Period, as a race of fishermen. During the Neolithic and Bronze Periods, the people in the remote inland areas remained primitive much longer than those living in more populated coastal regions. In the eighth century A.D., the Viking Period, Scandinavian society was well organized enough so that people undertook long sea voyages for conquest and colonization.

The visitor of today can expect to find some of the most beautiful scenery in the world, ranging from the mountains, glaciers, and fjords to the flat farmland and rolling hills near the lakes. Almost any venture will bring you near water in a lovely setting. The geological development and history of each region are detailed in many fine museums, where the traditions, costumes, and crafts of the people are also exhibited. The Scandinavian peoples love hiking, sailing, skiing, cycling, fishing, and the outdoor life in general. They have developed a very high standard of living, efficient transportation systems, and excellent medical and recreational facilities for everyone. The prices may be high (particularly in Sweden, less so in Norway, and moderate in Denmark) but by camping the traveler can afford to enjoy this beautiful part of the world. Scandinavia is not as jammed with tourists as the countries in Central Europe; it is still unspoiled, peaceful, and full of natural beauty.

Specifically, the national tourist offices in each country are trying to encourage visitors to camp because that is the best way of enjoying the landscape and meeting the people. A letter will bring you maps, a list of camping sites, pamphlets with all sorts of information about museums, shopping, seasonal events, and a collection of beautiful photographs to whet your appetite. Camping sites are clean, pleasant, and have more than the usual number of amenities. Camping fees are reasonable, and Scandinavian campers are often friendly and very likely to speak English. Mountain roads are usually open from late May or early June until October. When you find an area you like especially, you may want to stay longer.

Ideally, the itinerary that follows could be spread over a

longer period of time; it could be extended by several weeks to include the more remote regions of northern Norway and Sweden. You may prefer to omit some sections and spend more time in others; we discourage one-night stands and suggest that you plan to stay for several days in each campsite, relaxing and enjoying the munificence of natural beauty

DAYS 1, 2: COPENHAGEN

"Wonderful, wonderful Copenhagen. . . " and it is! Most visitors love everything about **Copenhagen**, from Hans Christian Andersen to Danny Kaye's lilting song. It is a city to have fun in, apart from remembering those fairytales heard in childhood. *Tivoli*, an amusement park located in the center of Copenhagen, is like a child's dream world. It is also the biggest bargain in Europe. For the price of admission you can spend all day and all evening until midnight enjoying performances or sitting and watching the world go by. Despite the fact that 40,000 persons stroll through the gates every day, the grounds look fresh and green, with fountains spraying and flowers blooming. You can enjoy concerts every evening, traditional pantomime, ballet with internationally renowned performers in the open-air theater, a marionette theater, and fireworks. The Tivoli Boy's Guard, similar to the King's Royal Guard, marches through the park with its own band. There are a number of restaurants on the grounds, not inexpensive but loaded with atmosphere. (Tivoli is open from May 1 through mid-September.)

The *National Museum*, on Fredericksholms Kanal, has archeological collections ranging from the Stone Age to more recent times, including Viking ships, folklore exhibits, and coin collections. *Christiansborg Castle* has royal reception rooms as well as ruins under the present castle. Bishop Absalon, who was well known for his ingenuity in fighting pirates, built the first castle as a fortress on that spot. The changing of the guard takes place every day at noon at *Amalienborg Palace*. Inside the palace you may see a collection of royal possessions spanning the years from 1863 to 1947. *Rosenborg Palace*, near the *Botanical Gardens*, houses the Danish crown jewels, as well as tapestries and china. You can take a canal and harbor tour from *Gammel Strand*, a marketplace, to *Langelinie* to see the statue of the *Little Mermaid* from Hans Christian Andersen's fairytale. We almost always buy smørbrod and walk to the Little Mermaid for lunch as we did the first time with Danish friends. The *Arsenal Museum* houses a collection of armor, weapons, uniforms, and battle flags. The *zoo and zoological gardens* contain a play zoo, and a structure that looks like a Chinese pagoda; you can ride up in it for a fine view from the top.

For excursions out of Copenhagen try *Dyrehaven*, a deer park near **Klampenborg** (you can also swim there). At **Lyngby** you will find an open-air museum in a 40-acre park called *Frilandmuseet*, where Danish farms have been reconstructed and are fully furnished with authentic pieces; there are also folk-dancing demonstrations. We particularly recommend *Louisiana*, a lovely modern art gallery with much sculpture outside in beautifully landscaped settings. It is north of the city near Klampenborg along the pleasant coast road to **Helsingor** (Elsinore). Here you will find *Kronborg Castle*, famous as the setting for *Hamlet*, which lives up to its reputation; it also contains the *Mercantile and Maritime Museum*.

In our opinion, shopping in Copenhagen is unrivaled. The main shopping street, *Stroget*, is closed to traffic, so you can wander back and forth with great pleasure. We always wish we had more time for shopping there. Everyone on our gift list has received either silver jewelry, wooden candlesticks, bowls, or trays purchased from small shops along Stroget.

Camping sites in Denmark are pleasant and easy to locate. There are 511 sites approved by the National Camping Committee of Denmark, six of which are in the Copenhagen area.

DAY 3: COPENHAGEN/ÖLAND, SWEDEN
(236 miles/378 kilometers)

Drive from **Copenhagen** on E4 to **Helsingør** and take one of the ferries to **Hälsingborg**, *Sweden*, or take a longer ferry directly from Copenhagen to Mälmo. Take E6 through **Malmö**, E14 to **Ystad**, 20 to **Kristianstad**, and 15 to **Kalmar** for the bridge (the longest in the world) to **Öland**. This route takes you along the Baltic coast of southern Sweden through fishing villages and small resorts, with many half-timbered houses in Ystad and a castle in Kalmar. There are seven campgrounds on Öland. Most have beaches with swimming and excellent facilities.

ALTERNATE ROUTE

For those who want to push on to **Stockholm** in one full day of driving, the main line is E4 from **Hälsingborg** through **Jönköping** on *Lake Vattern* and **Norrköping**.

DAY 4: ÖLAND

Öland contains archeological remains, at least one hundred old fashioned windmills, *Borgholm Castle, Solliden*, which is a chateau used during the summer by the Royal Family, fine beaches, and wildlife. You can take a ferry to **Gotland** and explore **Visby**, known as "The City of Ruins and Roses," following years of rich trade, subsequent ruin, and rediscovery. There are relics and ruins all over the island. Vilhelm Moberg, the author of *The Emigrants, Unto a Good Land*, and *Last Letter Home*, began his saga of emigration near **Kalmar**. There are many campgrounds on Öland.

DAY 5: ÖLAND/STOCKHOLM
(236 miles/378 kilometers)

Leave **Öland** via the bridge to **Kalam** and take 15 to **Norrköping**, then E4 into **Stockholm**. There are several campgrounds in Stockholm, all run by the municipality. You can camp outside the city in pleasant suburbs, such as **Sollentuna** or **Bromme**; in **Eskilstuna** to the west; **Västerås**, northwest of Stockholm; or **Uppsala** to the north on the large lakes (*Mälaren*) just west of the city, or on the Baltic coast to the east. Of the more than 500 campgrounds in Sweden, more are listed as first-class than in any other Scandinavian country.

DAYS 6, 7, 8: STOCKHOLM AND AREA

Stockholm, the "Venice of the North," is an expensive city to live in but worth the price for the treasures you can enjoy as a visitor. It developed from a fortress on an island at the junction of *Lake Mälaren* and the *Baltic*, became a town in 1250, and expanded to the present city of fourteen islands. The *Old Town*, also known as the "City Between the Bridges" or *Gamla Stan*, centers on the *Stortorget* (Great Square), which is near the *Royal Palace*. The Stockholm Massacre took place here in 1520 when ninety-four Swedish noblemen were arrested by the king and beheaded; their heads were piled in a pyramid in the middle of Stortorget. There is a changing of the guard at the *Royal Palace* every day at noon and some of the rooms in the palace are open to the public. Inside the *Storkyrka* (Great Church) you will find a painted woodcarving of St. George with the dragon, given to the church in 1489.

Across the inner harbor, the *Stadshuset* (City Hall) is a beautiful example of modern architecture with lovely mosaic walls in gold inside. Joining a guided tour at the appointed time is well worth the trouble. You will enjoy a perfect view of Stockholm if you are willing to undertake the long but interesting climb through various stages leading to the top of the tower.

Djurgarden (Deer Park) is situated on an island that is 2¼ miles long and ½ mile wide. Originally an enclosure for deer, the park now contains a wealth of interesting places to visit. *Skansen* is a favorite. As an open-air museum, it represents all of Sweden through reconstructed houses and shops, churches, farmhouses, rune stones, and a number of buildings from estates. Crafts are demonstrated, including glass-blowing, weaving, spinning, and book-binding. Entertainment includes folk-dancing in traditional costumes, folk operas, fireworks, and a Punch and Judy show. You can wander by a Lapp Camp and see the reindeer, or sit and enjoy watching the peacocks strutting about on the grass. There is also a zoo on the grounds. The *Nordic Museum*, by the North gate of Skansen, has collections that illustrate the development of Swedish civilization from the sixteenth century.

Nearby is the *Wasa*, a Swedish man-of-war sunk in the harbor by a freak squall just after she had been commissioned in 1628. This oldest intact ship of the seventeenth century, loaded with elaborate carvings, is in the process of being restored and preserved. She was raised from the harbor mud in 1961 and has since been bathed in preservative liquids to keep her from drying out and falling to pieces; the humidity is decreased slowly year by year. There is a marvelous museum with all sorts of details about the raising and preserving process. This was as fascinating to our son at 6 as it was when he was 16, and is interesting to adults as well. A film is also shown. For those interested in ships and the sea, the *National Maritime Museum* is also interesting.

Outside Stockholm you can visit *Drottningholm*, the favorite winter palace of the royal family, located on an island in Lake Mälaren. The ceiling paintings are impressive, as are the tapestries. *Drottningholm Court Theater* is next to the palace; eighteenth-century plays are performed here.

Just across the water from Stockholm lies the island of **Lidingö** and the home of the famous Swedish sculptor Carl Milles. *Millesgården* was purchased in 1906 and developed into a beautiful studio and home, which have been given to the Swedish nation. Milles' statues are placed inside, as well as in the carefully terraced garden leading down to the water. Milles was also a collector of sculpture and paintings, so both the wealth of fine work and the magnificent setting make this a memorable spot to visit.

Saltsjöbaden is one of the most popular year-round resort areas; tennis, swimming, sailing, horseback riding, and golf are available. It is located on a lovely Baltic fjord (*Baggensfjörd*) southeast of Stockholm. It is also possible to take boat trips out into the archipelago to visit some of the 25,000 pine-covered, rocky islands that sprawl eastward from the city proper. Here the water is warm and has so little salt that one can almost drink it. City dwellers take to their boats and may camp anywhere on private property as long as they remain a reasonable distance from summer houses. **Sandhamn**, on the eastern edge of the archipelago, is one major center of Swedish yachting on the Baltic. The Royal Swedish Yacht Club arranges international races there in the summer.

There are also many more museums, castles, and cathedrals to visit in the area surrounding Stockholm. **Uppsala** was the center of

Sweden until the late thirteenth century. In 1273 the archbishop settled there and the king moved to Stockholm; *Uppsala Cathedral* was begun around 1285 and finished in 1435; the University was founded in 1477. *Old Uppsala* is 2 miles north of the present city; the huge burial mounds there (dating from 500 A.D.) may contain the bones of pre-Christian kings.

DAY 9: STOCKHOLM/OSLO, NORWAY
(267 miles/427 kilometers)

Take E18 all the way to **Oslo**, passing through **Värmland**, the province that is the setting of Selma Lagerlöf's books (*The Wonderful World of Nils* and *The Saga of Gösta Berling*), through **Karlstad** on huge *Lake Vanern*, part of Sweden's inland waterway, and through the rugged timbering country on the Swedish-Norwegian border.

We have stayed several times in a large campground located west of the city on a lake. Many facilities are provided. There are several others in the Oslo vicinity. If you don't mind a drive, there are any number of campgrounds on both sides of the Oslofjord and to the west of the city in **Kongsberg, Drammen,** and **Svelvik**.

DAYS 10, 11: OSLO

Oslo is situated in a spectacular location at the end of the 60-mile-long *Oslofjord*, with mountains rising on both sides. The natural beauty of Oslo and all of Norway never ceases to entice those who love mountains and the sea. Water is never far away and people whose livelihood depends indirectly on the ships in the harbor can also enjoy the beauty of the fjord, swim in it, sail on it, and eat its delicacies. You can buy a bag of freshly cooked shrimp on the waterfront in Oslo or as you wait for ferries to cross the many fjords that make car travel through Norway slow but delightful.

For those who enjoy the sea, Oslo is full of maritime exhibits. In the *Viking Ship Museum* there are three long ships that were apparently used as burial chambers. The *Gokstad Ship*, 76 feet long, was a seagoing ship and is less ornate than the others. Warriors' shields were displayed over the gunwales as the ship was sailed or rowed on voyages in the Baltic, the North Sea, and the Atlantic. The *Oseberg Ship*, 70 feet long, originally contained the remains of a Viking queen, horses, dogs, a bed, a loom, clothing, cooking equipment, and a young servant girl buried alive. The *Tune Ship* consists of only a few pieces of the ship's bottom. *Kon-Tiki*, the balsa-wood raft sailed by Thor Heyerdahl from Peru to Polynesia in 1947, is on display with diaries and records of the trip. The ship's complement included five other men and one parrot. The *Fram*, the ship that carried Nansen to the Arctic in 1893 and Amundsen to the South Pole in 1910, is preserved with equipment and rigging intact.

The *Norwegian Folk Museum* includes an open-air collection of 150 wooden buildings arranged in courtyard groupings representing various provinces of Norway. The twelfth-century stave church from Gol, beautifully carved, is there. Henrik Ibsen's study is on exhibit, along with other Norwegian cultural collections. *Frogner Park*, located in the northwestern edge of Oslo, houses *Vigeland Sculpture Park and Museum*. Gustav Vigeland contracted with the city of Oslo to create a sculpture garden in the park. In forty years he completed 1,650 sculptures with the aid of assistants and workers. The results are very controversial but impressive, because he tried to create the cycle of human life in bronze and stone. Pathos, joy, agony, and other emotions are depicted in the nude figures. During the year of his death (1943), a gigantic monolith over 50 feet high and comprising 121 intertwined human figures was completed. The *Rådhuset* (City Hall) is a large red brick building with two towers. Both modern and lavish, it is decorated with paintings and sculpture done by contemporary Norwegian artists. The city also offers a number of art museums including the *National Gallery*, the *Munch Museum*, and the *Henie-Onstad Museum*.

There are several spots for a panoramic view of the Oslofjord and the city. One is *Holmenkollen Tower*, which was used in the 1952 Winter Olympic Games and is the most famous ski jump in Europe; a sports museum adjoins the tower. *Tryvannstarnet*

Tower has the highest elevation in Oslo and overlooks many square miles of fjords and towns. One may also enjoy the view looking up at the mountains by taking boat trips on the Oslofjord.

DAY 12: OSLO/SOGNEFJORD
(202 miles/323 kilometers)

Take E68 through **Hönefuss**, **Fagernes**, and **Laerdal** to **Revsnes**. There are spectacular views all along this route. Then take a ferry to **Kaupanger** and choose a campground in the area. Campgrounds are dotted along the fjord from **Skjolden**, **Gaupne**, **Höyheimsvik**, **Luster**, and **Sogndal** on the *Lustefjord*, which is an arm of the *Sognefjord*. To the west there are campgrounds at **Viksdalen**, **Balestrand**, and **Vangsnes**. Along the edge of the fjords the roads are narrow and curvy; in the mountains they are often steep. Visitors towing trailers should get a copy of *Motoring in Norway*, available from the Norwegian National Travel Office, which gives information on road conditions.

DAYS 13, 14: SOGNEFJORD AREA

Sognefjord, the longest fjord in Norway, stretches from the sea 125 miles inland to the foot of the *Jotunheimen* mountains. In places the mountains rise as much as 2,000 feet straight up from the water, and the fjord is as deep as 4,000 feet in some spots. The mountains northeast of the Sognefjord were christened "Jotunheimen" (home of the giants) by the poet Vinje; they are the highest mountains in Norway. *Jostedal Glacier*, the largest ice and snow area in Europe, can be compared with the gigantic icecap in Greenland. The top is 6,686 feet above sea level, the ice is between 1,300 and 1,600 feet thick, and it covers an area of 385 square miles. Twenty-six glaciers lead down into the valleys. Take the road to **Jostedal** and continue on to **Kroken** to a toll road leading to **Nigardsbre,** where you can play on the glacier. If you have time, go on over the highland tundra to **Lom** and turn west toward **Loen**. On the north side of Jostedal Glacier you can reach the *Briksdalbre Glacier* by turning at Loen. The walk in is about a mile but worth it for the spectacular view. The glacier rises from an ice-blue lake with small icebergs floating in it. Or, as an alternate expedition, take a ferry to **Flam** across the Sognefjord and ride the *Flamsbane*, said to be the most expensively constructed electric railway in the world. Within 12 miles it ascends 3,000 feet with a gradient of 1 in 18. There are spectacular views, tunnels, loops, and waterfalls to enjoy.

DAY 15: SOGNEFJORD/HARDANGERFJORD
(51 miles/82 kilometers, excluding ferry to Gudvangen)

Take the ferry from **Kaupanger** to **Gudvangen** for a magnificent crossing. Gudvangen is at the end of the *Naerøyfjord*, a branch of the *Aurlandsfjord*, which is in turn a branch of the Sognefjord. The approach to Gudvangen is increasingly shadowy and dark as the mountains become higher and closer together. Sheer drops provide more waterfalls than one can count easily; sometimes in the winter the sun is not visible in the fjord. As you leave Gudvangen, upon reaching the top of the gorge, look back at the view of the hairpin turns and amazing drops you have just navigated. Take E68 to **Voss**, an ancient town rich in peasant culture. The oldest standing house in Norway, *Finneloftet*, was built here in 1250. You might be lucky and watch a wedding procession lining up outside the thirteenth-century church, with everyone in traditional dress. Northwest of the town there is a ski lift, and the lake provides swimming and sailing. Continue on E68 to **Kvanndal**, where it is very pleasant to camp on the Hardangerfjord or one of its branches. Campgrounds are located in **Ringöy, Ovre, Eidfjord, Kinsarvik**, and **Lofthus**. (To reach those on the southern shore of the fjord, take the ferry from Kvanndal to Kinsarvik.) Most have marvelous views of the mountains along the fjords. Here you must decide whether you wish to spend more time hiking and exploring the fjords or would prefer city time in **Bergen**. You can reach Bergen for day trips from fjord campsites, or you can find campsites closer to the city on E68.

DAYS 16, 17: KVANNDAL/BERGEN and return
(71 miles/114 kilometers each way)

King Olaf Kyrre founded Bergen in 1070, Germans inhabited it starting in 1236, and commercial development began after 1343 with the rise of the Hanseatic League. Fishing and trade have been the sources of prosperity in Bergen. Artistic talent brought fame to Bergen through *Ole Bull* and *Edvard Grieg* in music, *Bjørnstjerne Bjørnson* and *Henrik Ibsen* in literature. The funicular leading almost straight up the mountain to *Fløyen* will give you a marvelous view of the city and the waterfront. The panoramic view must be one of the most beautiful anywhere; it is a perfect spot for lunch. *Bryggen* is composed of wooden warehouses built 250 years ago along the wharf. The houses are long, narrow, timbered, and gabled, all jammed together so that daylight barely has a chance to enter. *Torget* is a fish market at the end of the quay. The *Hanseatic Museum* is also in the same vicinity with exhibits about the merchants from the fourteenth to the seventeenth centuries on display. (You can see a set of scales used when a merchant bought goods and a separate one used when he sold goods.) *Gamle Bergen,* an open-air museum at *Sandviken,* has a number of old houses that had been removed from Bergen proper before a series of fires devastated the city.

DAY 18: KVANNDAL/STAVANGER
(107 miles/171 kilometers)
Take the ferry from **Kvanndal** to **Kinsarvik.** Drive on 47 to **Skare,** on E76 to **Haugesund,** and on 14 to **Skudeneshavn,** where you can take the ferry to **Stavanger.** Alternatively, take E76 from **Skare** to **Roldal** and 520 to **Sauda,** where you can take a longer ferry to **Stavanger.** (In choosing which route to take, decide how much you want to drive and how much you want to go by sea down the fjords. It is also possible, although more expensive, to take the ferry all the way from Bergen to Stavanger.) You will find a campground in Stavanger and another in **Sandnes** to the southwest. Others are located further south on the shore.

DAY 19: STAVANGER
Stavanger, the "Sardine Capital of the World," is one of the oldest towns in Norway. The old town, dating from the ninth century, is a fine collection of gabled houses, cobblestone streets, winding alleys, and busy markets. *Stavanger Museum* houses an-

tiques, exhibits on the natural history of the area, and a nautical museum. *Ledaal Manor*, once the Kielland estate (named for a novelist who died in 1906), is now a royal residence. The *Cathedral*, built in the eleventh century, is one of two medieval churches in Norway (the other is in **Trondheim**). You can take a boat trip into the *Lysefjord* to "The Pulpit" (1,800 feet above the fjord) for a spectacular view. Near *Viste* there are cave dwellings from the Stone Age.

DAY 20: STAVANGER/KRISTIANSAND
(162 miles/259 kilometers)

Drive through the plain of **Jaeren**, one of the few flat areas in Norway, on E18 to **Kristiansand**. King Christian of Denmark founded Kristiansand in 1641. *St. Olov's Cathedral, Christiansholm Fort, Gimle Castle, Møllevann*, a folk museum, and *Kongsgard*, a royal mannor turned into a school, are of interest. There are also excellent trout streams in the area. There is a campground in the southeastern part of the city that has fine facilities. Many others are available all along this popular resort shore.

DAY 21: KRISTIANSAND/ÅRHUS
(101 miles/162 kilometers, excluding ferry)

Take the ferry, a five-hour trip, from **Kristiansand** to **Hirtshals**, *Denmark*. Drive on A14 through **Alborg** to **Randers**, A10 to **Arhus**. There are many campgrounds in Jutland, along the sea as well as in the interior. The sand beaches of Jutland are among the finest in Europe.

DAY 22: ÅRHUS

Den Gamle By (the old town) is an open-air museum containing old town houses and shops grouped together to form a village. The shops have trade signs and are equipped with tools of the period. Weekly concerts are given during the summer in the *Cathedral of St. Clement*, which was founded in 1201. This is Scandinavia's longest church and is visible for miles. The *Town Hall*, which opened in 1941, provides a sharp contrast with its unusual architecture, a 200-foot tower, and a great deal of glass. The *University*, founded in 1928, has a 37-acre campus and is interesting architecturally. At **Moresgaard**, south of Arhus, you can see the 1,600-year-old Grauballe Man who was discovered in a peat bog, as well as other exhibits of prehistoric culture. There are also fine beaches nearby for a day of relaxation.

DAY 23: ÅRHUS/ODENSE
(74 miles/118 kilometers)

Drive from **Arhus** to **Odense** via E3, E67, E66 and A1. *Hans Christian Andersen*, a favorite storyteller for most children, was born in Odense in 1805. Besides visiting the bronze statue in the Hans Christian Andersen Park you can visit his birthplace on Hans Jensenstraede 39; this is now a museum housing his sketches, correspondence, school notebooks, furniture, clothing, and manuscripts of his fairytales. His childhood home on Munkemollestraed is also open to the public. There is a monument to King Canute in the market square. His bones were interred in a crypt in *St. Knud's Church* after he was murdered by pagans in 1086.

North of Odense, in **Ladby**, is a 1,100-year-old Viking ship (72 feet long) which was discovered in 1935. A Viking chief was buried in this ship around 900 A.D. with all his possessions, including four dogs, eleven horses, and many jewels. *Den Fynske Landsby*, south of Odense, is an open-air museum containing nineteen buildings including an inn, a weaver's house, mill, farm, hospital, and a theater that presents Andersen plays for children in the summer.

Many campgrounds can be found on the island of **Fyn**, all close enough to enjoy Odense.

DAY 24: ODENSE/COPENHAGEN
(83 miles/133 kilometers)

Take E66, a ferry from **Nyborg** to **Korsør**, A1 and A4 into **Copenhagen**. You may enjoy finishing your tour in a familiar city. There will be pleasures you did not have time for before you left the city more than three weeks earlier, and you may want more time for shopping there.

Summary

Our family completed this trip once as a whole and two or three times in sections. We found that 24 days allowed us to finish the entire route, but we spent more time driving than we prefer. As we traveled we stored memories for more leisurely future trips in our favorite areas. Those who like to explore more slowly would find it pleasant to spend several weeks in one country or region.

CENTRAL EUROPE

From Amsterdam: Paris, Geneva, Italian lakes, Milan, Florence, Pisa, Siena, Rome, Sorrento, Capri, Pompeii, Paestum, Amalfi Drive, Venice, Innsbruck, Heidelberg, Koblenz, Cologne, Amsterdam.

(35 days: 2,580 miles/4,128 kilometers = plan 1,2; 2,745 miles/ 4,392 kilometers = plan 3)

This trip has been planned to allow for minimum stays in each area of particular interest. It covers a lot of ground but the countries visited are close together and connected with auto routes for quick, easy travel. Those who wish to explore some areas further or to stop for special interests or sports can add extra days to the itinerary or omit entire regions (for example, by truncating the itinerary to cut off the Italian peninsula south of Rome or Florence). In several cases optional routes are listed to satisfy differing interests. (If you prefer secondary routes, allow a great deal more driving time, particularly in mountainous areas.) On each route you will find more interesting places to visit than you may be able to enjoy comfortably. Making choices as you go along is part of the fun of travel, and you will undoubtedly discover delightful stops that we missed entirely.

We have listed cities of historical interest on the itinerary, but that does not mean that you have to camp *in* them. We usually select campgrounds outside cities—they tend to be less congested and noisy—and drive or take some form of public transport into the city for each day's activities. We have also planned very few one-night stands, which means more to those traveling with tents than with campers. In most of the areas (for example, Sorrento) there is much to see and do that can easily be reached on day trips. By setting up camp for several nights you eliminate having to spend time searching for a suitable campsite, and a base camp allows you to relax in a temporary home where you know the ropes.

Visiting seven countries which contain enough variety to fill a

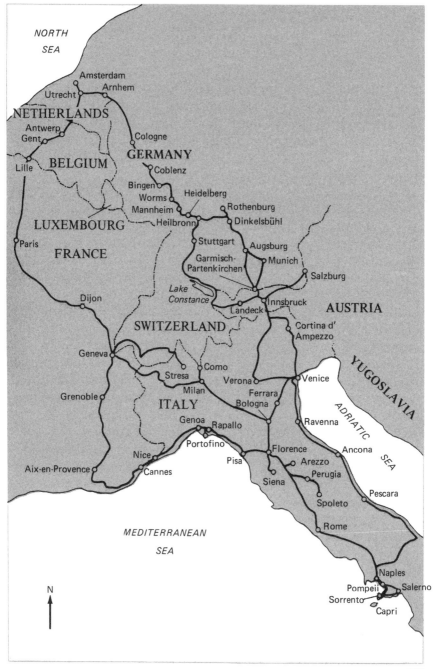

NORTH
SEA

NETHERLANDS

Amsterdam
Arnhem
Utrecht

Antwerp
Gent
Lille

BELGIUM

Cologne

GERMANY

Coblenz

Bingen
Worms
Mannheim
Heilbronn

Heidelberg

Rothenburg
Dinkelsbühl

LUXEMBOURG

Paris

FRANCE

Stuttgart
Garmisch-
Partenkirchen

Augsburg
Munich

Salzburg

Dijon

Lake
Constance

AUSTRIA

Landeck Innsbruck

SWITZERLAND

Cortina d'
Ampezzo

Geneva

Como

Stresa
Milan

Verona

Venice

YUGOSLAVIA

Grenoble

ITALY

Ferrara
Bologna

Genoa Rapallo

Ravenna

ADRIATIC

Portofino

Florence

Ancona

SEA

Nice

Pisa

Arezzo

Aix-en-Provence

Cannes

Siena

Perugia

Spoleto

Pescara

MEDITERRANEAN

Rome

SEA

Naples

N

Pompeii
Sorrento

Salerno

Capri

lifetime of travel forces you to be selective. It is particularly important that you write to the national tourist office of each country for information. Collect additional maps from other sources and plot your choices, leaving some room for a change of plans when you will fall in love with a place and want to stay longer. Since you cannot expect to become fluent in seven languages as you prepare for this trip, take along brief phrase books; if you do speak some German or French, either will serve as a back-up language in most regions. Enjoy!

DAYS 1, 2: AMSTERDAM

Amsterdam, a city of canals, can be seen and enjoyed best by boat. As the city developed outward, circular canals were added so that cargo could be brought from the Indies into the center of Amsterdam. Most of the tall, slender row houses have a beam extending from just above a large door in the top floor, where a block and tackle was once hooked to haul up goods from the barges below. These gabled houses have a variety of interesting roof shapes, some of them resembling stair-steps, that individualize them; don't forget to look up. Four hundred bridges link the narrow roads between the canals, but traffic is slow and congested.

Amsterdam is really a city for cyclists. Everyone—businesspeople, students, nuns, mothers with babies—cycles. There are special rooms set aside for the storage of bicycles throughout the city, and bikes can be taken on trains and into houses. At rush hours, cyclists outnumber pedestrians and motorists on the street.

In 1204 a castle was built on the site of Amsterdam. In 1578 the city gained its freedom from Spanish domination and began to grow as Ghent and Antwerp declined, doubling its size within a century as trade with the Dutch East Indies grew. From the middle of the seventeenth to the middle of the eighteenth centuries, Amsterdam was the center of European commerce until the vast resources of the British Empire shifted power to London. More than a century later, the North Sea Canal (built in 1875) and the Merwede Canal, which connected Amsterdam with the Rhine (completed in 1892), reinforced Amsterdam's advantageous position for trade in modern Europe.

The name *Amsterdam* came from the dam built at the junction of two rivers, the Amstel and the Ij. In one of the wettest places anywhere, a dam was successfully constructed and the main square laid out on top of it, called the Dam. The city center is still called the Dam. The *National Monument* to Dutch victims of World War II is in the center; soil from the eleven provinces of the Netherlands and from Indonesia was placed in twelve urns that stand there. On the west side of the square lies the *Royal Palace*, built in 1665. It is used only for receptions several times a year, because the Royal Family lives in Soestdijk near **Utrecht**, a residence that was given to Queen Juliana as a wedding present. In the northwest corner of the Dam is the *Nieuwe Kerk* (New Church) which dates from the fifteenth century. In East Amsterdam you will find *Rembrandt's house*, built in 1606, which holds a collection of his drawings and etchings. The *Rijksmuseum*, founded in 1808, contains a collection of old Dutch masters, led by Rembrandt, Steen, de Hooch, Van Dyck, Ruisdal, Hals, and Vermeer. There you may see *The Night Watch*, one of the most famous paintings in the world, which Rembrandt completed in 1642. There are also collections of porcelain, earthenware, sculpture, engravings, furniture, stained glass, and much more in the Rijksmuseum. In 1973 a nearby modern building, the *Van Gogh Museum*, opened; it houses an outstanding collection of his work. In an old residential section of Amsterdam, the Anne Frank House has been preserved. A number of Jews lived in hiding there during World War II, and you can see the bookcase that could be moved out to reveal a tiny stairway leading up to the rooms above where Anne Frank wrote in her diary.

There are many interesting side trips from Amsterdam. The *Kröller-Müller Museum*, located in *Hoge Veluwe National Park* north of **Arnhem**, is famous for the Van Gogh paintings and drawings on display there; other artists whose works are collected include Picasso, Mondrian, Seurat, and Braque. There is a modern gallery indoors and a lovely English garden which displays sculpture outdoors. The world's largest open-air flower exhibition, *De Keukenhof*, is located at **Lisse** (southwest of Amsterdam and south of **Haarlem**). It is open from the end of March until mid-May, with displays by bulb-growers covering 70 acres attractively arranged with pools containing black swans, sculptures, a windmill, and many greenhouses on an old estate in a natural woodland setting. There are other bulb fields to be seen all over Holland throughout the spring.

Near **The Hague** you can visit *Madurodam*, a Holland-in-miniature which contains buildings constructed on a scale of 1 to 25. This fascinating place includes many houses, a harbor with a lighthouse, canals, railroads, an airport, an amusement park with merry-go-rounds and ferris wheels, windmills, churches, and an opera house. The walking route is 2 miles long and all buildings are numbered. Authentic old Dutch villages where the townspeople may wear their traditional clothing daily and maintain most of the customs of their forefathers include **Spakenburg**, **Giethoorn**, and **Staphorst**. Visitors are not as welcome on Sundays in Staphorst because the townspeople are very pious and do not want others to stare as they walk in two separate files to church. **Marken** and **Volendam** may have been authentic once but now are tourist meccas overlaid with the usual extraneous trappings. A visit to parts of the *New Land*, which has been growing since the completion of a huge dike in 1932, is very interesting. This dike, the Afsluidijk, turned the *Zuiderzee* into a lake, now called **Ijsselmeer**. Hundreds of thousands of acres of land have been reclaimed by subsidiary diking and pumping out of water. The land in one northern section was pumped in 1942 and is now settled and tillable. The eastern section was completed in 1957 and the southern in 1968. You can drive completely around the Ijsselmeer, visiting former seaport villages still unspoiled by tourism.

There are 2,000 campgrounds in Holland, several in the Amsterdam area. One located near the airport is in a pleasant forested area. There are others located in towns to the north such as **Uitdam**, **Monnickendam**, and **Edam**.

DAY 3: AMSTERDAM/PARIS
(306 miles/490 kilometers)

Take E9 to **Utrecht**, E37 to **Breda**, E10 to **Antwerp**, and E3 to **Ghent**, which makes a nice lunch stop. Ghent is a lovely old Belgian city with medieval architecture and a fine arts museum. Then continue on E3 through **Lille** to **Paris**; there are a number of campgrounds located in and near Paris, including *Maisons-Laffite*, *Confians Ste. Honorine*, *Nesles-la-Vallée*, *Asnières-s-Olse*, and *Ermenonville*. Some are placed in semirural chateau towns like **Chantilly** (north), **Versailles** (west), and **Fontainbleau** (south).

DAYS 4, 5: PARIS

The Parisii, a tribe of Celts, built a fortress in the middle of the *Seine* on what is now called *Ile de la Cité*. The town spread through the surrounding forest and by the twelfth century Paris was a center of Western culture. The *Sorbonne* was founded in 1253. In succeeding centuries the city walls were extended, buildings and monuments rose, Napoleon brought back art treasures from his conquests, and the *Louvre* developed. French art, literature, and science made Paris the intellectual capital of Europe.

You can not hope to "see" *Paris* in a matter of days, but you can enjoy enough to make you want to return. Take a bus tour of the city and then go to the areas you are especially interested in on foot. Or take a tour on the *Seine* by boat. Or orient yourself with a bird's-eye view from the top of the *Eiffel Tower*. Then ramble as you wish through a section of the city, enjoying its pleasures— shops, sidewalk cafes, galleries, book stores, fine restaurants— slowly. The Metro is the quickest and cheapest way to get from one section of the city to another. *Nôtre-Dame*, an enormous grey stone Gothic cathedral on Ile de la Cité, was started in 1163. From across the Seine the size, pinnacles, gargoyles, and flying buttresses are most impressive. As you approach the west facade you will see a number of sculptures on the doorways, including the Last Judgment in the center with a figure of Christ in triumph. Above the north door is a series of niches containing the Kings of Judah

(28 statues.) The rose window, begun in 1230, is 31½ feet in diameter and served as a model for similar windows in other cathedrals. Inside, the light from the rose window illuminates statues and the lovely carving on the choir screen. Climb the 252 steps to the Grande Gallerie and 80 more up to the South Tower for a sweeping view of Paris. Nearby *Sainte Chapelle* also has beautiful stained-glass windows and mosaic work. The *Conciergerie*, once a medieval palace, served as a prison during the Revolution. Marie Antoinette, Robespierre, Madame du Barry, and André Chénier waited there until they went to the guillotine.

The *Right Bank* of the city refers to the expensive and fashionable section north of the Seine. Walking from east to west, begin at the *Louvre*, probably the most famous museum in the world, where you can see *Venus de Milo*, *Winged Victory*, *Mona Lisa*, and more paintings, sculpture, and art objects than you can assimilate in a week. The *Tuileries Gardens*, developed in the sixteenth century for Catherine de Médici, who wanted an Italian Renaissance garden, are decorated with pools and sculptures. Rectangular in shape, they border the Seine, and cover 60 acres of central Paris. The *Jeu de Paume* is a Louvre annex containing Impressionist paintings, and the *Orangerie* hangs the work of post-Impressionists and has special exhibitions. Next you will come to the *Place de la Concorde*, one of the largest and most impressive squares in the world. Along with fountains and an obelisk, the square once held the guillotine. On your left you will see the *Petit Palais*, containing art collections, and the *Grand Palais*, a large exhibition building. Continue on the Champs Elysées to *Arc de Triomphe*, the largest arch in the world, where twelve avenues meet in the center of the star. The grave of the unknown soldier is in the center, with a flame burning day and night. The arch is decorated with a sequence of sculptures depicting the glory of France. Climb the 280 steps to the top for a fine view of Paris. To the north *Montmartre*, once a village for artists and writers, now is a tourist mecca. Its hill is crowned by the basilica of *Sacre Coeur*, a large white Romanesque/Byzantine structure that dazzles the eye.

The *Left Bank*, south of the Seine, is more student-oriented, cheaper, and has a Bohemian atmosphere. The *University of Paris*, the *Sorbonne*, is located in the *Latin Quarter*. *St. Julien le Pauvre*, the University's first chapel, is now a Greek Orthodox church. *St. Séverin* is a beautiful late Gothic church with impressive stained-glass windows. The *Phantheon* is the burial spot of Victor Hugo, Rousseau, Voltaire, and Zola. *Hotel de Cluny*, a mansion built by the Abbots of Cluny, is now a museum of medieval art objects which features rare tapestries. The *Palais du Luxembourg*, built for Marie de Médici in 1620, is now the meeting place of the French Parliament, and the adjoining *Jardin du Luxembourg* is a park containing many sculptures and monuments. The *Hôtel des Invalides* contains the tomb of Napoleon surrounded by oversized columns and figures; his statue is 8½ feet tall, which is 3 feet 4 inches taller than he really was. Farther west is the *Tour Eiffel*, built by Gustave Eiffel in 1889 for the World's Fair. Although considered too "modern" and only temporary when it was built, it is still there for flocks of visitors to enjoy. Brief excursions outside the city proper will bring you to the overwhelming palace of *Versailles*, the grand chateau at *Fontainebleau*, or the more modest chateau at *Chantilly;* all are surrounded by formal gardens, and the last two adjoin extensive forest tracts that originally were hunting preserves.

DAY 6: PARIS/GENEVA
(300 miles/480 kilometers)

Take E1 until it meets 5 near **Dijon**, then 5 through **Dijon**, **Dole**, and **Poligny** into **Geneva**. Alternate routes: stay on the E1 to **Châlon-sur-Saone**, then take 978, 78, and 5 to Geneva; or stay on the E1 farther south to **Lyon** and take the E46 to Geneva. The last part of all three routes is slow but interesting driving over the Jura mountains. Campsites are available along the lake toward **Nyon** and **Lausanne** in **Vesenaz**, **Mies**, **Tannay**, **Morges**, **Cully** and **La Croix-s-Lutry**.

DAY 7: GENEVA AND AREA

Lake dwellers chose the site of **Geneva** for their home as early as 4000 to 5000 B.C. The left bank of the River Rhône became the center of the town. In the fifth century Geneva became a bishopric; the *Cathedral of St. Pierre* was built between the tenth and thirteenth centuries. John Calvin arrived in 1536, turning the city away from entertainment to rigid austerity during the Reformation. Geneva is now the home of the International Red Cross, the International Labor Office, and The World Health Organization. It is a cosmopolitan and international center of world renown.

In a lovely setting on *Lac Leman* is the *Palais des Nations*, which was originally the home of the League of Nations; notice the beautifully sculptured sphere in front. You may want to wander around the cobblestone streets of the *Old Town*. It surrounds the *Cathedral of St. Pierre*, which is plain but impressive. You can climb the north tower for a view of the entire region—Geneva, the Jura Mountains, Lac Leman, and the Alps. During the summer, concerts and plays are given in the courtyard of the *Hôtel de Ville*, a sixteenth-century building. You can also take boat trips to **Nyon** a lovely town with a medieval castle, or to the *Château de Chillon*, near **Montreaux**. Francois Bonivard, who displeased the Duke of Savoy, was cast into the dungeons at the castle and lived chained to a pillar for four years. Byron visited the castle in 1816 and wrote the lyrical poem about Bonivard which made the castle famous.

DAY 8: At this point in the itinerary you must choose between the pleasures of three alternative routes, each full of mountains to enjoy:

DAY 8, PLAN 1: (ITALIAN LAKES VIA LAC LEMAN AND SWISS ALPS) GENEVA/STRESA
(190 miles/304 kilometers)

Take N1 to **Lausanne**, N9 and E2 along the Rhone River valley and through the tunnel under the *Simplon Pass* (or E2 over the pass in foul weather), then 33 to **Stresa**. All of the Italian lakes are teeming with campgrounds.

DAY 8: PLAN 2: (ITALIAN LAKES VIA FRENCH AND ITALIAN ALPS)
GENEVA/COMO
(200 miles/320 kilometers)

Take E21B by the north face of *Mont Blanc* and through the tunnel under it to **Aosta**, then E21 and A5 to **Ivrea** (north of **Torino**), A4 to **Milan**, and A9 to **Como**.

DAY 8, PLAN 3: (FRENCH AND ITALIAN RIVIERA VIA FRENCH ALPS AND PROVENCE)
GENEVA/AIX-EN-PROVENCE, FRANCE
(223 miles/357 kilometers)

Take E4 and A41 through **Chambéry** to **Grenoble**, 75 and 96 to **Aix-en-Provence**. Several campgrounds are located a few miles east of town, and one is to the north.

DAYS 9, 10, PLANS 1 AND 2: ITALIAN LAKES AREA, MILAN

We would be inclined to visit the Italian lakes and settle in for a time, omitting the hassle of sightseeing in large cities. The lakes of Lombardy are unbelievably beautiful, with snow-capped mountains reflected in deep blue water, lemon trees planted amidst villas, promenades where you can sit and sip coffee or have an Italian ice, gardens everywhere, sailboats on the lakes, and warm sunshine even in winter. *Lago Maggiore* is 40 miles long and contains the **Borromean Islands**. The most famous of these, *Isola Bella* (Beautiful Island), looks like a wedding cake with its tiers and terracing. **Stresa**, a town on the western shore, was once a fishing village and is now an international resort. You will want to take a boat trip to enjoy the full variety and beauty of the lake. To the east beyond *Lago di Lugano*, a narrow mountain lake with handsome villas on the north shore, is *Lago di Como*, set between towering mountains to the east and west. It is 30 miles long and divides into two legs at its southern end; because roads are narrow and slow, it is best to see the lake by boat. Much farther to the east, *Lago di Garda*, the largest lake in Italy, is 32 miles long and 11 miles wide, with lowlands in the south and a beautifully engineered lakeside road in the more mountainous northern end. The climate is warmer there because the lake is sheltered from cold north winds by the mountains. To supplement the natural beauty of the Italian lakes, there are castles, cathedrals, and museums all over the region.

Milan, today a progressive and volatile commercial city, still holds some of the treasures of the past, including the *Last Supper* located in the *Cenacolo Vinciano*, next door to *Santa Maria delle Grazie*. The *Duomo*, located in the center of Milan, is one of the largest cathedrals in the world. It is built in the shape of a Latin cross and is a wonderful maze of spires, gables, and sculpture; you can walk up onto the roof for a closer look at the statues. The renowned opera house, *La Scala*, built in 1779, has an enormous chandelier suspended from the frescoed ceiling, as well as a museum.

DAYS 9, 10, PLAN 3: AIX-EN-PROVENCE/PORTOFINO
(229 miles/366 kilometers)

Take A8 to **Cannes**, **Nice**, **Monte Carlo**, and A10 through **Genoa** to **Portofino**. The *Côte d'Azur* extends from **Marseilles** to the Italian border, the Italian Riviera from **San Remo** to **La Spézié**. The mild climate and mountainous coastline, dotted with beautiful sand beaches and lush vegetation, have made this area of the Mediterranean an international playground for the wealthy. You may want to stop and enjoy the atmosphere at Cannes, Nice, and Monte Carlo. Less affluent travelers will also enjoy the benign climate and rugged scenery of the coast as a welcome break from city sightseeing. The eastern section of the Italian Riviera is full of wonders, including marvelous ports like Portofino (with *Rapallo* high above the sea), La Spézié, and **Lerici**. Camgrounds are plentiful all over the Riviera.

DAY 11, PLANS 1 AND 2: ITALIAN LAKES/FLORENCE
(215 miles/359 kilometers)

From **Milan** take A1 to **Bologna**, E6 to **Florence**.

ALTERNATE ROUTE

Take the A7 to **Genoa**, the E1 and A12 to **Pisa**, and the E55 and A11 to **Florence** (suggested if you want to stop in Pisa).

DAY 11, PLAN 3: PORTOFINO/FLORENCE
(118 miles/189 kilometers)

Take E1 and A12 to **Pisa**, E55 and A11 to **Florence**. There is a campground in Florence near *Piazzale Michelangelo,* two more in pleasant country settings in **Fiesole** (north), and another just south of the city.

DAYS 12, 13, 14: FLORENCE, PISA, SIENA, HILL TOWNS

Florence grew from an Etruscan village into a city flourishing with trade guilds by the eleventh century. In the thirteenth century the Guelphs appeared as supporters of Rome's popes against emperors who tried to gain power. Florence grew and prospered, led by shrewd and honest bankers who became influential all over Europe. The Médici regime gave splendor to the city through the arts for three centuries. The Italian Renaissance was born in Florence, through the sculpture and painting of Michelangelo, da Vinci, Rossellino, Bartolommeo, Botticelli, Ghiberti, Donatello, Pisano, Cellini, Giotto, Masaccio, Fra Angelico, and Lippi, and the writing of Dante, Machiavelli, Petrarch, and Boccaccio. A number of central books in Western culture are associated with Florence. Among them are Dante's *The Divine Comedy;* Machiavelli's *The Prince;* and, more recently, Henry James' *The Portrait of a Lady.* In 1944 Hitler's troops blew up all the bridges in Florence except the *Ponte Vecchio* (Old Bridge) as they retreated northward during the Italian campaign. In 1966 a flood swept through the city, covering treasures with mud; people all over the world contributed money and time in an effort to salvage them.

We have always enjoyed leaving something to see for our next trip to Florence, selecting what we want to do very carefully and savoring the experience. You may want to orient yourself first by studying maps and then by enjoying the panoramic view from the *Piazzale Michelangelo,* located on a hill above the city. The center of this remarkable city is small enough to be surveyed by eye and comfortably explored on foot. You will want to dispose of your car in the outskirts because the center of the city is congested and has very little parking.

Piazza Del Duomo (Cathedral Square) contains the *Cathedral of Santa Maria del Fiore*, begun in 1296 and finished in 1434. The spectacular exterior is covered with variegated white, green, and red marble; in comparison, the Gothic interior seems stark, bare, and enormous. You can climb up to the inner gallery of the dome for a view of the cathedral nave and outside onto the top of the dome for a panoramic view of Florence. The stained-glass windows were made from the work of Donatello, Uccello, and Ghiberti. In the first chapel in the north transept you can see the unfinished pietà which Michelangelo worked on at the age of 80. And underneath the cathedral the ruins of an older tenth-century cathedral have recently been opened. Giotto designed the accompanying 269-foot *campanile* in the fourteenth century. There are 414 steps to the top, which offers another panoramic view. Facing the front of the *Duomo* is the *Battistero*, with huge gilt doors famous all over the world. The south door contains the work of Andrea Pisano done in 1330 and is Gothic in style; the north door, done by Lorenzo Ghiberti from 1403 to 1424, depicts the life of Christ; the east door, also by Ghiberti, illustrates scenes from the Old Testament. This door, said by Michelangelo to be worthy of the Gate to Paradise, lost five panels during the 1966 flood; all have since been found and restored. Inside the Battistero there is a thirteenth-century mosaic covering the ceiling (which can be lit if you request it).

Piazza Della Signoria is an open-air sculpture gallery containing *Perseus Holding the Head of Medusa*, by Cellini; *Judith and Holofernes*, by Donatello; a copy of *David*, by Michelangelo; *Neptune*, and *Hercules* and *Cacus*, by Bandinelli. The *Palazzo Vecchio* (Old Palace) contains paintings and sculptures, the apartment of Eleanor of Toledo, wife of Cosimo I, a Médici, and the town hall. The *Uffizi Museum*, in a Renaissance palace, is the richest museum in Italy and one of the finest in the world. You will have to choose what you would like to see among the superb collections. The *Pitti Palace and Gallery* on the other side of the *Ponte Vecchio* (Old Bridge) houses more priceless art treasures. The *Boboli Gardens*, a beautiful example of Italian terraced gardens, are just outside the Pitti Palace. Admirers of Michelangelo (and readers of

Irving Stone's *The Agony and the Ecstacy)* may want to continue searching for more of Michelangelo's work in the *Medici Chapel*, where you will see the figures of *Dawn, Dusk, Night,* and *Day,* or in the *Accademia Gallery* to see the original statue of *David.* There are many, many more museums, churches, and statues to see if you have the desire and the stamina. You will want to stroll slowly across the *Ponte Vecchio* bridge with its shops, and the *Mercato Centrale* is an experience for shoppers who like to bargain for sweaters, leather goods, and straw pieces.

There are a number of day trips that are convenient from Florence. **Siena** is famous for a wild horse race, the *Palio delle Contrade,* held in the *Piazza del Campo* every July 2 and August 16. The Piazza del Campo looks like a giant scallop shell and is elaborately paved with red brick and white stone in patterns. Contestants and officials all wear medieval costumes, and participants are allowed to lash each other as well as the horses. The *Duomo* is located on the tallest hill of the three Siena is built on. It was begun in 1065 and completed during the fourteenth century, and has unique paving done by a number of artists over a period of two centuries. The *Cathedral Museum* contains the *Maesta of Duccio* as well as *The Three Graces.*

Pisa, founded as a Greek port although the coast is now 6 miles away, is the home of the *Leaning Tower,* a campanile with the top 14 feet off the vertical because of a slip of land during construction. You can climb 294 steps to the top for a fine view (the guardrails at the top leave a lot to be desired for the not-so-brave); if you do climb try *not* to go up just before the hour because the bells will nearly make you want to jump off. Galileo used the cathedral to study the pendulum, and the leaning tower to work on laws of gravity and the acceleration of falling bodies. The *Duomo* was built in marble of alternating colors; inside, the pulpit, shaped as a polygon, contains a series of pillars with statues depicting the Virtues.

The landscape south of Florence toward Siena and **Rome** is spotted with hill towns (many of them walled), with beautiful winding streets and ancient buildings. Many of them also contain art treasures that are not to be seen anywhere else. If you have time, you will want to visit **San Gimignano, Lucca, Arezzo, Perugia, Assisi,** or **Spoleto**.

DAY 15: FLORENCE/ROME
(162 miles/259 kilometers)

Take A1 all the way to **Rome** unless you choose to explore some hill towns along the way. There are some campgrounds in Rome, and many in outlying areas from the sea to the west (**Ostia**) to one near Hadrian's Villa in the east (**Tivoli**).

DAYS 16, 17: ROME

Rome is large enough and complex enough to overwhelm the visitor. Driving is almost always frustrating and can be terrifying, and pedestrians take their lives in their hands when they set foot into a street. We found crossing the broad circular street around the Coliseum to be a real game of chance (even worse than trying to drive around the Arc de Triomphe in Paris). The noise, traffic, pollution, and the squalor of some sections can be depressing but should not make you skip the historic and artistic treasures of Rome. We have appreciated the city more by camping in outlying calm, peaceful settings to restore our battered senses. And we quickly learned *not* to drive during the four daily rush hours.

According to legend, Romulus (one of the twin sons of Mars who was suckled by a she-wolf until a shepherd found them) traced the walls of the city in 753 B.C. and forbade anyone to cross the line. His twin brother, Remus, violated the injunction and was killed. (A live female wolf kept in a cage at the steps of *Capitoline Hill* perpetuates the legend.) However, there was probably a Stone Age settlement on the site long before Romulus and Remus. Before The Roman Republic, an Etruscan King, Servius Tullius, believed in democratic government but was overthrown. Some of the art of the Etruscan period can be seen in the *Etruscan Museum* in the *Villa Giulia*. In 509 B.C. the Roman Republic was established, ruled by the Senate and Consuls. After 390 B.C., when the Gauls invaded and sacked Rome, she was ravaged again periodically. The Republic was replaced by the early Empire under

Octavius, with the title of Augustus Caesar, from 27 B.C. until Nero burned most of Rome in 64 A.D. Marcus Aurelius later reunified the Empire and had many buildings erected that are still standing in Rome. The later Empire continued from 283 to 476 A.D. before it was overwhelmed by barbarian invasions and diminishing resources. Gradually pagan buildings in Rome were converted to Christian uses; even the Pantheon was consecrated in 609. The Holy Roman Empire was founded in 962 A.D. by Otto I, former King of Saxony, leading to centuries in which Christian Rome was the center of church and state, but the modern political unification of Italy as a nation had to wait until the nineteenth century. Throughout all these vicissitudes, Rome has remained the symbolic center of Christianity and much of Western civilization.

The *Roman Forum*, located between the *Piazza Campidoglio* and the *Palatine*, was once the center of Roman life during the Republic. Excavations during the nineteenth and twentieth centuries have uncovered temples, prisons, an arch, and many other buildings. The *Palatine* is a continuation of excavated ruins, including gardens, houses, and a palace. The *Coliseum*, opened in 80 A.D., takes its name from the "colossal" statue of Nero that stood there; here gladiators fought and early Christians were thrown to the lions in early forms of public entertainment. The *Pantheon*, started in 27 B.C. by Agrippa, has an impressive dome and represents the accommodation of classical Rome to the needs of the Holy Roman Empire.

Vatican City, the smallest state in the world, is located on a hill west of the *Tiber River* and is separated from Rome by a wall. Since 1929 it has been an independent state, having its own coins, newspaper, postage stamps, and radio station. The population is about 1,000; about 500 of these are soldiers dressed in uniforms designed by Michelangelo. *St. Peter's,* begun in 319 A.D., is the largest church in the world. As you stand in the square you will be in an ellipse formed by two semicircles of Doric columns extending out as arms of the church. The dome, created by Michelangelo, is supported by four gigantic pillars. You can climb up into the dome, or take an elevator, for a panoramic view of Rome. In the first chapel on the right you will see Michaelangelo's *Pietà*, sculpted when he was 22 years old. It is now protected against vandalism by reinforced glass. The *Vatican Museum* is housed in a series of palaces and contains the largest collection of art treasures in the world. The *Sistine Chapel* may be the climax of your stay in Rome. Michelangelo's *Last Judgment*, on the end wall, and his frescoes on the ceiling cannot be adequately described; they must be seen.

The other delights of medieval and Renaissance Rome are too numerous to detail here. Those who want to explore the city in depth should plan to stay for five to seven days.

DAY 18: ROME/SORRENTO
(152 miles/243 kilometers)

Take A2 and A3 beyond **Naples** to **Castellammare di Stabia,** then 145 onto the *Sorrento Peninsula.* Campgrounds are frequent but expensive along this coast. The greatest concentration of campgrounds in fine settings occurs just beyond the town of **Sorrento** and in **Massalubrense.** We enjoyed one located in an orange grove overlooking the sea.

DAYS 19, 20, 21: CAPRI, AMALFI DRIVE, PAESTUM, POMPEII

The Sorrento Peninsula is high on a cliff overlooking the *Tyrrhenian Sea;* it divides the *Gulf of Naples* from the *Gulf of Salerno.* It is an ideal spot for both doers and sitters: there is much to visit and much to enjoy in the warm sun on this spectacularly beautiful peninsula.

Just off the end of the peninsula lies the **Isle of Capri,** a paradise discovered by ancient Romans. It can be reached by boat from Sorrento for a day trip. You will not want to leave, however. Capri is composed of two gigantic rock masses with a cleft in the middle. Much of the coastline is high, jagged, and completely inaccessible by boat. In between these pinnacles of rock there are grottos and a startingly blue sea. The vegetation is lush and prolific. We enjoyed spending most of our time on the island taking walks through the areas that are wildest, particularly the coastline south of the village of Capri. (You can buy a little guide in the village with these walks clearly marked.) We have found that the walks often take longer than we plan, possibly because we pause so frequently to look down the cliffs to the surf below. You can also go into the *Blue Grotto* by boat when the sea is calm. We also recommend taking the bus to **Anacapri** and riding the chairlift up to the summit of *Monte Solaro*, where the view encompasses the island, the Sorrento peninsula, and the whole of the Gulf of Naples, including the city and Mount Vesuvius beyond.

The *Amalfi Drive*, the corniche road that follows the coast from **Sorrento** to **Salerno**, is one of the most breathtaking roads anywhere. The mountainside, with its vineyards and villages tilted toward the vertical, and the narrow, curvy, hairpin turns so far above the sea make the drive appealing and frightening. If you have a choice, avoid taking this magnificent drive on weekends and holidays when it may be full of traffic. We spent a great deal of time at each narrow turn one Easter weekend while tour buses maneuvered back and forth trying to pass. This encounter was repeated over and over until one bus driver would either give up and back up, along with all the traffic behind him, or get out and wave his arms, with additional theatrics from drivers of nearby cars or pedestrians, until a compromise was reached. In any case, each spot was lovelier than the last. The rugged rocks, gorges plunging to the sea, hillsides sprinkled with orange and lemon trees, flowers everywhere, and people picnicking on a beautiful day defined the essence of an Italian holiday. There are a number of towns along the coast including **Positano, Praiano, Vettica, Maggiore, Minore, Amalfi**, and **Maiori**. Don't miss a short but steep side trip to the mountain town of **Ravello**, which has a piazza overlooking the whole coast. And if you are interested in pottery, stop in **Vietri**, the last village before Salerno.

Paestum, originally Poseidonia, is located about 20 miles south of Salerno. It was an ancient Greek seaport city, dating back to the sixth century B.C., which fell into ruin because of an outbreak of malaria. The temples that remain are built of fine yellow limestone, with massive pillars in contrast with the green vegetation that has grown up around them. The *Temple of Neptune*, perhaps misnamed because it was probably dedicated to Hera (Juno), has fourteen columns lining the sides; six are across the ends of a massive structure 200 feet long. The *Basilica* is the oldest temple in Paestum and was also dedicated to Hera; it has fifty fluted Doric columns. The *Temple of Ceres* consists of thirty- four columns still standing, and contains a sacrificial altar. The *Archaeological Museum* houses the contents of Greek tombs, including paintings.

Pompeii, founded in the fifth century B.C., was covered by the eruption of *Vesuvius* in 79 A.D. Pliny described the scene: a strong earthquake in the morning, followed by smoke and a shower of cinder which covered the ground 3 feet deep. Some fled, some stayed indoors; then a second rain of molten lava and cinders covered the town. In 1748, during the reign of Charles of Bourbon, excavation was undertaken. The streets have high curbs with stepping-stones across at corners (with gaps for chariot wheels, which have left ruts). The buildings are made of brick with marble and plaster overlaid. The center of life in Pompeii was the *Forum*, a square paved with marble flagstones. On it, the *Temple of Jupiter* was the most important place of worship; the *Basilica* was used for judicial and business affairs. There are two theaters, a large and a small, a gymnasium, and public baths. The houses and villas reflect many styles: the *House of Vettis* has well preserved frescoes and an Etruscan garden with statues; the *Tragic Poet's House* has a mosaic of a dog tied with a chain; the *Lucrezio Frontone House* contains mythological paintings; the *House of the Large Fountain* has lovely mosaic wall decorations; the *House of Venus in the Shell* is named after a mosaic depicting Venus sailing in the shell, escorted by two Amoretti; the *Loreio Tiburtino's House* has more mythological paintings, a stream with waterfall, fountains, and statues in the garden; and the *Villa of Mysteries* contains a freize that may depict the initiation rites of one of the Dionysian cults that flourished in Pompeii. The *Antiquarium* displays items that have been uncovered, including human and animal bodies preserved by lava. After you have explored the city, you can drive and then walk up to the crater of Vesuvius to see where it all began. There are two roads up the mountain: the one on the north side is paved and less precipitous. The rim overlooking the crater is narrow and will probably pump some adrenalin into your system (no guardrails).

DAYS 22, 23: NAPLES/VENICE
(433 miles/693 kilometers)
Take the A2 to **Rome**, A1 to **Bologne**, A13 to **Ferrara** and **Padua**, and the A4 to **Venice**. Alternate route: Take A17 across the boot until it joins the A14, then follow the coast of the *Adriatic Sea* north to **Rimini** and turn toward **Ravenna**, which is worth a stop if you have time. Camp on *Punta Sabbioni* (to the east of Venice), where there are fine beaches and many campsites to choose from. It is easy to take a ferry into Venice and perhaps safer to leave your car and belongings there than on the other side in **Mestre**.

DAYS 24, 25: VENICE
Although the early history of Venice is obscure, the earliest settlers may have been Romans seeking refuge from their Lombardian conquerors in the islands of the lagoons. The first Doge was probably Paulucius Anafestus in the eighth century A.D. In 809 A.D. King Pepin, the son of Charlemagne, sailed up into the lagoons but was repulsed. By 819 Angelus Participotius, the Doge at that time, was living on the site of the present Palace of the Doges. Venice was growing and developing as a link between the Byzantine and Franconian empires to the east and west. In 828 the body of St. Mark was brought to Venice; his symbol, the winged lion, was taken over and St. Mark became the protector of the town. During the Crusades, Venice made many conquests and became one of the most important of Italian powers. Marco Polo returned from his travels with riches in the late thirteenth century. Venice was at its height of naval and mercantile power in the fifteenth century until the discovery of America and new sea routes to India changed the pattern of world trade and brought decline to sea routes in the Mediterranean.

The relationship between Oriental commerce and the art of Venice is evident. *St. Mark's Cathedral* is an example of Byzantine style, and mosaics throughout the city reveal that influence. From the eleventh to the thirteenth century the architecture developed from closer Lombard-Romanesque sources, and from Gothic styles during the fourteenth and fifteenth centuries. In the last half of the fifteenth century the famous school of Venetian painting began to develop with Bellini, Giorgione, and Carpaccio. During the later Renaissance Titian, Veronese, and Tintoretto flourished there.

Venice lies almost 3 miles from the mainland in a lagoon protected from the sea by long sand-hills or *lidi*. Much as we might wish it otherwise, the sea is gradually destroying Venice; there are floods every year and Venice is slowly sinking. It used to be the custom to recognize this dependence on the sea. Every year on Ascension Day the Doge, elaborately dressed in gold, would sail out and throw a ring into the sea, saying, "We wed thee, Sea, in token of our perpetual rule." Voltaire commented that the marriage was not valid without the consent of the bride.

The most interesting and efficient way to explore Venice is by water. You can take a vaporetto (a water bus), a ferry, a water taxi, or a gondola, depending on where you want to go. You can have a fine tour of the Grand Canal at little cost by taking Line 1 of the vaporetto. In a gondola you can poke into narrow back canals, with or without the romantic trappings of commentary or serenade by the gondolier. (Be sure to bargain for your gondola hire before you step in, and hold to it when you pay. Then relax and enjoy your trip in one of the most graceful and efficient boats ever designed.)

Most visitors spend some time in *Piazza San Marco*, a gigantic square bordered by elaborate arcades sheltering shops and cafes on three sides facing the *Basilica San Marco*. You may want to pick up mail at American Express just off the square, collect some tourist guides and information, and settle down for a leisurely cup of espresso in an open-air cafe while enjoying the view. The Basilica, or Church of Gold, was originally built to hold the remains of St. Mark. In the Byzantine style, St. Mark's is a dazzling example of mosaic and marble combined. The facade is built around five doorways with a number of columns in between them, a gallery above, and one gigantic dome and four smaller ones on top. Inside, the mosaic work glitters with gold and brilliant colors.

The famous *Pala d'Oro* (gold altarpiece), made in 976 in Constantinople, contains diamonds, emeralds, rubies, and topaz. The *Treasury* contains the spoils of the Crusades and relics such as bones, skulls, goblets, and chalices. Up in the gallery is the *Marciano Museum*, which exhibits mosaics and tapestries. Outside you can have a close-up view of the Bronze Horses, taken to Paris by Napoleon and returned after the fall of the French Empire. Climb (or ride an elevator) up the adjoining *campanile* for a panoramic view of Venice.

Palazzo Ducale (Doges' Palace), built with pink and white marble in a geometric pattern above a Gothic gallery, looks like a gigantic birthday cake. It has a horseshoe shape around a courtyard adorned with sculpture. Inside you will see treasures of painting and sculpture, including works by Bellini, Titian, Veronese, and Tintoretto. The full tour of all the reception rooms, halls, and courts used in the administration of this city kingdom is well worth the time. The *Bridge of Sighs* unites the palace with the prison, giving prisoners a last glimpse of the Grand Canal as they passed over it to incarceration or death.

The much-photographed *Clock Tower* on the Piazza features two Moors, carved in bronze, who have been striking the hour for 500 years. Below them on the Tower stands the winged lion, the emblem of Venice, and below the lion, the Virgin and Child in copper. You can also climb this tower for an unobstructed view of the city.

There are many churches, schools, museums, and bridges to see, but you may prefer to just wander at will. It is easy and pleasant to be lost in Venice, even with map in hand. Each alley and square brings new discoveries, and some of the finest palazzi can only be seen from the canals. The most ardent shoppers will find more to look at than they can manage or afford, and world watchers will enjoy small cafes overlooking squares and canals. You may also want to spend time on the beaches of **Lido**, or take a boat trip to **Murano** to see glassblowers at work, to **Burano**, famous for lacemaking, or to **Torcello**.

Among the literary works about Venice are Goethe's *Italian*

Journey, Ruskin's *The Stones of Venice*, Henry James' *The Aspern Papers*, and Thomas Mann's *Death in Venice*.

DAY 26: VENICE/INNSBRUCK
(209 miles/334 kilometers)

DAY 26, PLAN 1:
Take A4 to **Verona**, A22 over the *Brenner Pass*, A13 to **Innsbruck**.

DAY 26, PLAN 2:
Take A27 to **Vittoria Veneto**, 51 to **Cortina d'Ampezzo**, then to **S. Candido**, 49 to **Bressanone**, A22 to the *Brenner Pass*, A13 to **Innsbruck**.

There are three campgrounds in Innsbruck and many more in the area, such as those located in **Uterperfuss**, 8 miles west; **Rinn bel Innsbruck**, 8 miles southeast; **Solbad Hall**, 8 miles east; **Volders**, 12 miles east; and **Weer**, 16 miles east.

Verona makes an interesting lunch stop or longer if you wish to track the lore of Romeo and Juliet or explore an ancient city. **Cortina**, the site of the 1956 Winter Olympics, is in an area of rugged beauty with pink shades appearing on the rock faces of the surrounding *Dolomites*; the drive beyond goes through some of the most interesting mountain scenery in the Alps.

DAYS 27, 28, 29: INNSBRUCK, GARMISCH, SALZBURG

Innsbruck (Bridge over the Inn River), capital of the Tyrol, remains one of our favorite cities anywhere. The beautiful mountains rise straight up from the city, to the north the Alps and to the south the mountains of the Tuxer range. In winter you can ski or ride chairlifts up for the view from a number of locations, including **Seegrube** to **Hafelekar**, **Igls** to **Patscherkofel**, **Seefelt**, and **Mutters**. In the summer hiking is available in big doses or small, in combination with the funicular or chairlifts.

At some point you will find yourself strolling along the *Maria-Theresien Strasse*, the main street. Look toward the north for a striking view of the *Nordkette*, which is the Northern Karwendel mountain range. At the southern end of the street is the *Triumphal Arch*, built in 1767 by Maria Theresia to commemorate the marriage of Archduke Leopold to Maria Ludovica and the death of Franz I, husband of Maria Theresia, events that happened at the same time. *Annasäule* (St. Anne's Column) is a monument halfway down the street, commemorating the birthday of St. Anne because the Tyrol was liberated from the Bavarians on that day in 1703. At the end of Maria-Theresien Strasse continue on down Herzog Friedrich Strasse to the end where you will see *Goldenes Dachl* (Little Golden Roof), built by Maximilian with golden coins. He used the balcony as a "royal box" when watching performances or tournaments below. *Hofburg Palace*, built by Maria Theresia on the site of an earlier fifteenth-century palace, contains paintings and ornate furniture. There is a lovely park there patterned after an English garden.

A number of day trips may be conveniently taken from Innsbruck. To the northwest is **Garmisch-Partenkirchen**, 35 miles away in Germany. This is an Alpine sports area with very colorful Bavarian murals painted on houses and hotels. You can take an electric railway and cable car to the top of the *Zugspitze* for a spectacular view of the Alps and for skiing (winter or spring) or hiking (summer and fall). To the northeast is **Salzburg**, 92 miles (154 kilometers) away in a beautiful setting on the banks of the *Salzach River*. It is also the home of the renowned Salzburg Music Festival, which runs from the last week in July through August. Wolfgang Amadeus Mozart was born in Salzburg in 1756; *Mozarts Geburtshaus* (Mozart's birthplace) at 9 Getreidegasse contains his violins, spinet, letters, and manuscripts. *Hohensalzburg*, the twelfth-century fortress above Salzburg, provides a fine view of the town. Dancing the Viennese Waltz on the terrace of the Cafe Winkler can be romantic for a 21-year-old or for anyone young at heart. There are many churches to visit in Salzburg, as well as the *Archbishop's Residence* and the *Glockenspiel*, with seventeenth-century bells on Residensplatz. Six miles away is *Schloss Hellbrunn* (Hellbrunn Castle), the summer residence of Archbishop Marcus Sitticus, who, with a delicious sense of humor, created hidden water jets all over the garden to surprise the unwary.

DAYS 30, 31: INNSBRUCK/ HEIDELBERG
(302 miles/483 kilometers)

Take 313, E6 to *Garmisch-Partenkirchen* and **Munich**, E11 to **Augsburg** (or, if you prefer more pleasant rural roads, 23 and 17 from **Garmisch** to **Augsburg**), then 25 to **Dinkelsbühl** and **Rothenburg**, back south to E12 through **Heilbronn**, and E4 to **Heidelberg**. There are several campgrounds upstream of Heidelberg on the *Neckar*. It is a noisy but interesting river.

Dinkelsbühl is a charming medieval town that merits an hour or two of strolling on the wide cobbled streets, climbing the Romanesque tower, and viewing the dungeons in the town hall.

Rothenburg ob der Tauber is another very picturesque medieval town that is well known to tourists. You can walk around it on the old wall as well as climb up into the 197-foot belfry. There are a number of museums and interesting buildings to explore.

ALTERNATE ROUTE

For those who have not had enough of lakes and mountains, take the E17 west through the **Arlberg**, the A14 north to the *Lake of Constance*, and the 31 along its shore, then the E121 through the *Black Forest* to **Offenburg**, E11 to one of the old spas of Europe, **Baden-Baden**, and the E4 north to **Heidelberg**.

DAY 32: HEIDELBERG

Heidelberg has a medieval town (enclosed in a larger modern city) with an enormous castle and Germany's oldest university. The castle, which rises above the town and the river, is now in ruins, and there is a rose-tinted cast to the stone; it could be the scene of a romantic operetta and, in fact, is during the summer. The castle was first built in the thirteenth century but was destroyed along with the town in 1689 during the Orleans War. Then, in 1764, the rebuilt castle was struck by lightning and has remained a ruin ever since, but a large part still stands with many interesting rooms, terraces, towers, and gardens to visit. You can also see the *Heidelberg Tun*, a gigantic cask dating from the eighteenth century. According to legend, its guardian, a dwarf named Perkeo, had a tremendous capacity for wine and was able to drain it to the last drop. In the town you can visit the *Studentenkarzer* (Students' Jail), where rowdy students carved inscriptions, their silhouettes, and coats of arms on the walls. The *Universitatsbibliothek* (Library) contains rare manuscripts, and there is also a beautiful old lecture hall with frescoes and carving preserved in the university.

DAY 33: HEIDELBERG/KOBLENZ
(95 miles/152 kilometers)

Take 67, 6 and 61 past **Mannheim** and **Worms**. At **Bingen** take 9 along the river on the west bank of the *River Rhine* (or, crossing by ferry, 42 on the east bank) to **Koblenz**. You will pass a number of castles: *Rheinstein, Reichenstein, Sooneck*, then legendary *Lorelei Rock*, where the river narrows and boats encounter whirlpools, captains perhaps bewitched by an enchantress who tries to lure them to their doom, and several interesting towns and villages. Camp outside the city in the Koblenz area and take a couple of hours to see *Marksburg*, a castle that looks and feels like a castle should. The rooms and furnishings give a good sense of the rugged quality of life in hilltop fortresses. You may want to take a steamer trip on the Rhine (leaving your car and returning to it by train), or at least cross on one of the little car ferries that link east and west banks. The vineyards, rocks, castles, and wooded hills make the area between Bingen and Koblenz the most pleasant stretch of the Rhine. There are many good campgrounds along all the Rhine, but most are very noisy because of the railroads, roads, and constant barge traffic.

DAY 34: KOBLENZ/AMSTERDAM
(216 miles/346 kilometers)

Take 61 to **Cologne**, where you will want to see the Cathedral, one of the finest in Europe. It took 600 years to build this magnificent cathedral. During World War II it was hit by so many bombs and shells that only the shell remained, but it has now been completely restored. Its 515-foot towers completely dominate the entire region; inside, the Shrine of the Three Magi, a twelfth-century work kept in a glass case behind the altar, is most striking in gold and silver. After your visit, take 3 to **Arnheim**, A12 to **Utrecht**, and A2 to **Amsterdam**.

Summary

We have traveled this basic route in 21 days with young children. With two teenagers we enjoyed the trip in 22 days. In our younger days two of us stretched it out to 35 days, but found camping that long exhausting. It *can* be done, but you may find it more enjoyable to cut some areas and pause to enjoy those you do visit longer. On the other hand, for a once-in-a-lifetime trip you may choose to see and do as much as possible. In planning a trip this long—really a camper's version of the old "grand tour of the continent"—you will have to weigh your own inclinations heavily in determining both the pace and the emphasis.

Skiing

It is possible to winter camp in the valleys near many European ski areas. However, if you can swing it, renting a flat (apartment) or chalet is very pleasant. You can still save a great deal of money by doing your own cooking, and by going during the low season (December until Christmas; January after the holidays; after Easter until June). There are a number of companies involved in renting Alpine flats. One of them, Swiss Chalets Inter Home (Buckhauserstrasse 26, CH-8048 Zurich, Switzerland), publishes a detailed book listing flats by area, including size, number of beds, linen, dishes, fireplace, balcony, and in some cases, a photograph of the building. The Swiss National Tourist Office in New York has copies of this book. We did some research on where we wanted to ski, thinking about the skiing skills of each family member, and then looked up accommodations by price in each area.

When we called Swiss Chalets in October, it was already too late to reserve one of the most desirable flats during high season. By keeping our children out of school one week after vacation we were able to take advantage of low-season rates and had a much wider choice of flats still available. Swiss Chalets was pleasant to deal with, both on the phone with the English office and when we arrived at the local office. We knew the terms and conditions when we arrived, had our deposit ready, and signed the inventory. The flat had more than enough sheets, towels, blankets, and pillows. The beds were comfortable and we each had plenty of drawer and closet space. The kitchen was well supplied with dishes and cooking needs; there were also laundry facilities in the basement of the building. Swiss Chalets made arrangements for a supply of wood to be delivered for the fireplace, which we enjoyed every night. We thoroughly enjoyed skiing and then returning to a pleasant home with a spectacular view, where we could relax and cook our own meals.

Choosing the perfect ski area is not easy, but you can't go far wrong in the Alps if you are careful about defining your own needs. The great variety of French, Swiss, Austrian, Italian, and German resorts available, each with its own atmosphere, terrain, and style of accommodations, makes your choice significant. Some big-name resorts cater to the international jet set and adjust their prices accordingly; others have trails suited only for experts; some, like the new French resorts, specialize in certain types of accommodations. It is easy to gather the information you need by writing for pamphlets or dealing with an agent who specializes in ski weeks. (But beware of being talked into an agent's "special" package in lieu of making your own arrangements; it will probably cost more unless you are able to do your own cooking.) To make your choice easily, decide (1) what range of difficulty in terrain your family wants; (2) what language you feel most comfortable with; (3) what region of the Alps has special appeal for you; (4) whether you want to stay in a "famous" resort or would settle for comparable skiing in a less well-known Alpine village; (5) how you want to get there—by car, train, or in some cases, funicular or cable car. Finally, you must decide how long you want to stay. We have always been sorry to leave after one week, but if you are blessed with more time, you might want to spend a week each in two or three resorts. Our choices have included the following resorts, which are well-adapted to family skiing:

CORTINA (ITALY): the site of the 1956 Olympics, where the downhill course plunges through a chute between two massive natural stone pillars; many lifts and connecting runs down into the town; a wide range of skiing available, from beginner to expert; an active night life in a town swarming with people on weekends; and lots of sun.

LECH (AUSTRIA): an excellent beginner's area and ski bowl in the village, with high and varied bowl skiing above; interlacing trails leading to Zurs and St. Anton for day trips; many long cable cars including one over a very spectacular gorge for half a mile; open snow fields at very high altitude almost completely above the tree line; beautiful spring skiing in bright sun (bring very dark glasses for the flat light); you may need chains on your car (a requirement to drive over some of the passes).

ZERMATT (SWITZERLAND): spectacular views of the Matterhorn; three different areas, serviced by lifts, ranging from sunny open snowfields facing the Matterhorn to skiing under the base of it; a very picturesque village with only sleigh or foot traffic, remote from the noise and confusion of the twentieth century; you will leave your car below Zermatt (in an area that is plowed and easy to drive to) and take a cog railway up to Zermatt; doing without a car is worth it when you can gaze at that amazing hunk of rock in all weather and from various angles.

VERBIER (SWITZERLAND): a huge high bowl facing in three directions, with the village at the bottom so it is possible to follow the sun throughout the ski day; many convenient lifts with frequent bus service free with your lift ticket; intermediate skiing in a high bowl at high altitude; expert skiing in many sections of the bowl; fine beginners' slopes at the edge of the village; Mt. Zele, an area for experts, serviced by a cablecar up to what seems like the top of the world; you can see into Italy and France from the station perched on a cliff, as well as ski into those countries.

Biking

Depending upon your skill, interest, and desire you may want to choose fairly flat terrain or challenging grades. You can fly your bicycle with you or rent one there, but if you plan to rent one you will want to make inquiries in advance. Also, if you are used to a good bike and might not be happy with rental equipment, you may be wise to bring yours along.

Holland is one excellent choice for bicycle touring. The land is flat, there are special bike paths beside most roads, and there is a wealth of lovely old houses, country estates, windmills, and interesting scenery. Roads in the "new land" are not heavily traveled and are unspoiled by tourists. You may want to plan a variable itinerary so you can ride with the wind at your back.

Backpacking

Backpacking is available and interesting in many mountain areas in Europe. You can buy your equipment after you arrive or bring it from home. However, you may prefer hiking in a pair of boots that have been broken in. You can write in advance for maps and guides, which are available in major bookstores such as Heffer's in Cambridge, Foyle's in London, or Blackwell's in Oxford. Also, write national tourist offices and local tourist information centers in the specific areas in which you plan to hike.

In England the *Pennine Way* is somewhat similar to the Appalachian Trail; it is a long trek down the spine of the country; you can stage hikes in sections. The *Lake District* varies in terrain from forested areas near Coniston to the moors of Ulswater and the rugged, barren wilds of the Langdale Pikes. *Snowdonia* provides pleasant walks to a crystal lake and many difficult climbs for the experienced. Scotland contains the same range of possibilities.

A source for English walking holidays is: Tom Harrison, *English Wanderer*, 13 Wellington Court, Spencers Wood, Reading RG7 IBN England.

The *Alps* contain a system of hiking trails and huts. You can ride lifts up or down and plan interconnected routes, spending nights either in mountain huts or in village inns. Write the tourist offices in areas of your choice.

Canal Boating

You can rent comfortable, self-contained houseboats by the weekend, week, or month. Travel by such boats creates relaxing, slowly moving days through pastoral countryside. You will have the fun of going through locks, sometimes operating them yourself, and some canals even go over roads on water bridges. Many waterways provide a maze of intricate wandering through the country.

In the center of England you can travel from **Stratford** to **Manchester** on the *Avon* and a further system of canals linking midland cities with one another. In the *Norfolk Broads* there is a series of canals linking small bodies of water called Broads and continuing to the sea; you can travel from **Norwich** to **Yarmouth** on this system. Write to tourist offices in those towns for information or to Hoseasons, Sunway House, Lowestaft, Suffolk, N R 32 3LT England.

Holland is interlaced with canals, and you can go completely across France by canal. Write the national tourist offices in each country for specific suggestions, and for more information on France, write to Horizon, 215 North 75th St., Belleville, Ill. 62223.

appendix

BOOKS TO READ BEFORE YOU GO

Cope, Bob and Claudette, *European Camping and Caravaning*, Drake Publishers Inc., New York, 1974. A book containing useful information to be used in the planning stages of a trip. Topics include various types of caravans, campers, and camping equipment, selected campgrounds, lists of national tourist offices, and much more.

Fielding, Nancy and Temple, *Fielding's Travel Guide to Europe* or *Fielding's Low-Cost Europe*, William Morrow & Co., New York, published annually. These guides have a wealth of general information written in a chatty style. They do not include history of the area, and suggestions for sightseeing are limited. The emphasis is on hotels, not camping.

Fodor, Eugene, *Fodor's Germany* (and any other country), David McKay Company, Inc., New York, published annually. These guides have excellent historical information. Some of the chapters are written by news commentators and other prominent people who have lived overseas. A great deal of specific information is included.

Frommer, Arthur, *Europe on $15 a Day*, or *Dollar-Wise Guide to Italy* (and others), Simon & Schuster, New York, published annually. This is one of the best guidebooks for sightseeing if the cities you want to see are covered. Many very helpful tips and facts, historical information, and readers' suggestions are included.

Hadley, Leila, *How to Travel with Children in Europe*, Walker and Co., New York, 1963. This is a source with a great deal of useful information for families traveling with young children and offers suggestions for sightseeing not found anywhere else. It also supplies helpful addresses and phone numbers.

Harvard Student Agencies, *Let's Go: Europe*, E. P. Dutton & Co., New York, published annually. Candid and concise sightseeing tips are covered from a student's point of view, as well as some camping and much general information. It is bulky with ads.

Holiday Magazine Travel Guides, Random House, New York, published annually. Interesting detail on sightseeing with good coverage of towns and cities, anecdotes, and historical information.

Lanier, Alison R., *Living in Europe*, Charles Scribner's Sons, New York, 1973. Excellent tips for those living in Europe for some time, including some only the locals know. Very helpful information to have before departing.

Martin, Lawrence, *Europe: The Grand Tour*, McGraw-Hill, New York, 1967. Interesting historical information about cities you will visit, written in a pleasant conversational style.

Michelin Green Guide (to every country), Jarrold & Sons, Ltd., Norwich, England. The most concise, detailed, complete guide available. Slim, easy to carry. Take it with you for areas of special interest.

Youth Hosteler's Guide to Europe, Macmillan, New York, 1977. Covers countries with maps, narrative, and sightseeing details.

LOCAL FOODS TO TRY

Austria

SOUP	Leberknödlsuppe (meat broth with liver dumplings) Gulaschsuppe (goulash soup with beef, onions, paprika)

ENTREE   Wiener Schnitzel (veal steak, breaded and fried)
                       Schweinefleisch mit Kraut (pork with cabbage)
                       Schweinefleisch mit knödel (pork with dumplings)
                       Tafelspitz (boiled beef)

DESSERT   Sachertorte (rich chocolate cake with apricot jam and
                       chocolate icing)
                       Strudel (dough with fruit)
                       Linzertorte (almond torte with ham)

CHEESE   Gruyère, Tilsit, Butterkäse

Denmark

SOUP   Rødgrød med fløde (jellied fruit soup with cream)

ENTREE   Kogt torsk (boiled cod)
                       Røget laks (smoked salmon)
                       Biksemad (beef tartare)
                       Frikadeller (meatballs)

DESSERT   Wienerbrød (Danish pastry)

CHEESE   Danish bleu, Danbo with caraway, Münster, Tybo,
                       Samsøe, Dofino

England

SOUP   Cock-a-leeky (chicken and leeks)
                       Oxtail
                       Scotch broth

ENTREE   Roast beef and Yorkshire pudding
                       Fish and chips
                       Steak and kidney pie

Toad in the hole (sausages in batter)
Bangers and mash (sausages and mashed potato)
Leg of lamb
Finnan haddie (haddock in white sauce)
Lancashire hotpot (lamb and vegetable stew)
Cornish pasties (beef and vegetable pies)

DESSERT   Trifle (spongecake, jam, pudding, sherry, whipped
               cream)
               Banbury cake (currant cake)
               Bath buns (raised dough with raisins)
               Fruit fool (puréed fruit with whipped cream)
               Syllabub (pudding)
               Dundee cake (fruit cake)

CHEESE   Stilton, Cheshire, Caerphilly, Double Gloucester,
               Leicester, Wensleydale

France

SOUP   Soupe à l'oignon (onion soup)
               Le pot-au-feu (beef and vegetable soup)
               Vichyssoise (potato soup)
               Bouillabaisse (fish soup)

ENTREE   Blanquette de veau (veal)
               Choucroute à l'Alsaçienne (sauerkraut and pork)
               Coquilles Saint-Jacques (scallops)
               Coq au vin (chicken in wine)
               Boeuf Bourguignon (beef stew)
               Carbonnade flamande (beef in beer)
               Escalopes de veau (scalloped veal)
               Chateaubriand (steak)
               Canard aux pommes (duck with apples)
               Quiche Lorraine (cheese pie)

DESSERT   Baba au rhum (yeast cake with rum sauce)
               Madeleines (tea cakes)

Les crêpes (pancakes)
Mousse au chocolat (chocolate mousse)

CHEESE   Brie, Boursault, Port du Salut, Roquefort, Camembert

Germany

SOUP   Linsensuppe mit mettwurst (lentil soup with sausage)
Kartoffelsuppe (potato soup)
Fleischbrühe (clear soup)
Hühner brühe mit nudeln (chicken noodle soup)
Obstsuppen (fruit soup)

ENTREE   Sauerbraten (beef marinated in vinegar, wine, spices)
Königsberger Klops (meatballs)
Fleischklösschen (meat dumplings)
Bratwurst mit Spätzle (sausage with noodles)
Hasenpfeffer (rabbit stew)

DESSERT   Napfkuchen (Bundt cake)
Stollen (Christmas bread with candied fruits)
Haselnusstorte (hazelnut torte)
Lebkuchen (gingerbread)
Streuselkuchen (crumb cake)

CHEESE   Münster, Limburger, Tilsit

Italy

SOUP   Minestrone (vegetable)
Zuppa di pesce (fish soup)
Stracciatella alla Romana (chicken broth with egg and cheese)
Pasta in brodo (pasta in broth)
Pasta e Fagioli (macaroni and beans)
Zuppa di Riso e Patate (rice and potato)

ENTREE	Scaloppine alla Marsala (veal with Marsala wine) Cioppino (fish stew) Pollo cacciatora (chicken with tomato) Scampi di vina (shrimp with wine) Veal Parmigiana (veal with Parmesan cheese)
PASTA AS AN ENTREE	Lasagna al forno (lasagna with meat) Cannelloni (noodle tubes filled with meat or cheese) Ravioli (square dough stuffed with meat) Spaghetti, Tortelloni, and other noodles
DESSERT	Zabaglione (custard with wine) Spumoni (ice cream with fruit) Gelati (ice sherbert) Panforte (sweet cake with almonds, fruit) Panettone (yeast cake)
CHEESE	Bel paese, Gorgonzola, Parmesan, Pecorino, Latticini, Mozzarella, Fontina, Provolone

Netherlands

SOUP	Erwtensoep (pea soup) Groentensoep (clear consommé with vegetables and meatballs)
ENTREE	Hutspot (vegetable stew) Maatjes herring (early herring) Rolpens met Rodekool (beef and tripe with red cabbage) Boerenkool met Rookworst (kale, potato, and sausage) Mosselen (mussels) Heete Bliksem (pork chops with apples)
DESSERT	Chocoladetaart (chocolate torte) Speculaas (St. Nicholas cookies) Banketletter (almond-filled cookie)

CHEESE   Edam, Gouda

Norway

SOUP   Sildegryn (herring)
                  Fisksuppe (fish)

ENTREE   Lutefisk (cod)
                  Fersk Suppe Og Kjött (soup with meat and vegetables)
                  Rendyrstek (reindeer)
                  Fiskeboller (ground halibut)

DESSERT   Tyttebaer (lingonberries)
                  Multer (cloudberries)
                  Julekake (Norwegian holiday bread)
                  Bløt Kake (layer cake served on Constitution Day, May 17)
                  Fyrste Kake (Prince cake)

CHEESE   Geitost, Taffel, Tilsit, Jarlsberg

Sweden

SOUP   Blandad Fruktsoppa (fruit soup)
                  Vitkalssopa (white cabbage soup)

ENTREE   Kotbüllar (meatballs)
                  Biff à La Lindström (beef and potato patties)
                  Kalops (braised short ribs)
                  Kalvrulader (veal rolls)
                  Smörgåsbord (a variety of hot and cold foods)
                  Kräftor (crayfish)
                  Kokt lax (boiled salmon)

DESSERT   Plättar (pancakes)
                  Sockerstruvor (rosettes)

Lucia Saffransbrod (Lucia buns)
Mandelformar (almond tarts)

CHEESE   Fontina Gräddost, Tilsit

Switzerland

SOUP   Kassuppe (cheese soup)

ENTREE   Berner Platte (bacon, sausage, ham, beef, sauerkraut, potato)
              Kalbsbratwurst (veal sausage)
              Geschnetzeltes Kalbsfleisch (minced veal with cream)
              Bündnerfleisch (dried beef)

CHEESE DISHES Fondue (cheese and wine eaten by dipping cubes of bread)
              Râclette (Valais cheese melted by a fire, eaten with potatoes and pickles)

DESSERT   Kirschenkuchen (cherry cake)
              Gugelhopf (poundcake)

CHEESE   Gruyère, Emmental, Appenzeller

CONVERSION TABLES

Clothing Size	American	British	Continental
women's dresses, suits, and coats	8	30	36
	10	32	38
	12	34	40
	14	36	42
	16	38	44
	18	40	46
women's blouses, sweaters	34	36	42
	36	38	44
	38	40	46
	40	42	48
	42	44	50
	44	46	52
women's shoes	6	4½	36
	6½	5	37
	7	5½	38
	7½	6	38
	8	6½	38½
	8½	7	39
men's suits, sweaters, coats	34	34	44
	36	36	46
	38	38	48
	40	40	50
	42	42	52
	44	44	54
men's shirts	14	14	36
	14½	14½	37
	15	15	38
	15½	15½	39
	16	16	40
	16½	16½	41

Clothing Size	American	British	Continental
men's shoes	9	8½	43
	9½	9	43
	10	9½	44
	10½	10	44
	11	10½	45
	11½	11	45

Weights

ounce	= 28.35 grams	1 gram	= 0.04 ounce
pound	= 0.45 kilogram	1 kilogram	= 2.20 pounds
ton	= 0.91 metric ton	1 metric ton	= 1.10 tons

Liquid Measure

pint	= 0.47 liter	1 liter	= 2.11 pints
quart	= 0.95 liter	1 liter	= 1.06 quarts
gallon	= 3.79 liters	1 liter	= 0.26 gallons

Length

inch	= 2.54 centimeters	1 centimeter	= 0.39 inch
foot	= 0.30 meter	1 meter	= 3.28 feet
yard	= 0.91 meter	1 meter	= 1.09 yards
mile	= 1.61 kilometer	1 kilometer	= 0.62 miles

Distance

Kilometer to miles:

1 kilometer	=	.62 miles
10 kilometers	=	6.20 miles
20 kilometers	=	12.40 miles
30 kilometers	=	18.60 miles
50 kilometers	=	31.00 miles

Miles to kilometers:

1 mile	=	1.6 kilometer
10 miles	=	16.00 kilometers
20 miles	=	32.00 kilometers
30 miles	=	48.00 kilometers
50 miles	=	80.00 kilometers

75 kilometers = 46.50 miles	75 miles = 120.00 kilometers
100 kilometers = 62.00 miles	100 miles = 160.00 kilometers
Multiply by .6	Multiply by 1.6

Gasoline

U.S. gallons:	to liters:
1	3.8
2	7.6
3	11.4
4	15.1
5	18.9
6	22.7
7	26.5
8	30.3
9	34.1
10	37.9

Temperature

To compute Fahrenheit: multiply Celsius by 1.8 and add 32.
To compute Celsius: subtract 32 from Fahrenheit and divide by 1.8.

Celsius		Fahrenheit
100	boiling point	212
90		194
80		176
70		158
60		140
50		122
40		104
37	normal body temp	98
30		86
20		68
10		50
5		41
0	freezing point	32

index

AA Guide to Camping and Caravanning on the Continent, 44
Aberdeen, Scotland, 106, 108
Aberfeldy, Scotland, 109
Airlines, 14–16, 68
Air mattresses, 24
Air Travelers' Fly-Rights, 68
Aix-en-Provence, France, 139
Alborg, Denmark, 127
Alcester, England, 95
Amalfi, Italy, 147
American Express, 11
Amsterdam, Holland, 27, 132–133, 156
Anacapri, Italy, 147
Anticipation of trip, 8
Antwerp, Belgium, 135
Aosta, Italy, 139
Arbroath, Scotland, 108
Archaracis, Scotland, 112
Arden, Scotland, 113
Arezzo, Italy, 144
Arhus, Denmark, 127–128
Arlberg, Germany, 154
Arnhem, Holland, 133, 156
Assisi, Italy, 144
Augsburg, Germany, 154

Austria, 152–153, 158–159, 164–165
Automobiles
  buying, 37–38
  leasing, 38
  renting, 36–38
  shipping home, 39
Avebury, England, 86
Aviemore, Scotland, 106, 109–110

Backpacking, 160
Bacon/baked beans recipe, 51
Bacon hash recipe, 51
Baden-Baden, Germany, 154
Bala, Wales, 95, 96
Baldock, England, 102
Balestrand, Norway, 124
Ballachulish, Scotland, 112
Ballater, Scotland, 109
Balmoral Castle, Scotland, 106, 109
Banking, 11–12
Bannockburn, Scotland, 113
Barnstaple, England, 85
Bath, England, 85–86
Beauly, Scotland, 110
Beddgelert, Wales, 95, 96
Beef stroganoff recipe, 51

Beers, 46–47
Belgium, 135
Benderloch, Scotland, 112
Ben Nevis, Scotland, 111, 112
Bergen, Norway, 125–126
Bergen soup recipe, 59
Betws-y-Coed, Wales, 96
Beverages, 46–47, 49
Bideford, England, 85
Biking, 159–160
Bingen, Germany, 155
Blackmore Gate, England, 85
Blair Atholl, Scotland, 109
Blenheim Palace, England, 88, 93
Bognor Regis, England, 81
Bologna, Italy, 140, 149
Borromean Islands, Italy, 139
Bosham, England, 81
Bournemouth, England, 83
Braemar, Scotland, 106, 109
Braunton, England, 85
Breda, Holland, 135
Bressanone, Italy, 152
Bridgewater, England, 85
Bridgnorth, England, 95
Bristol, England, 85
Broadford, Scotland, 110
Bromsgrove, England, 95
Bumping, 68
Burford, England, 87
Burton on the Water, England, 87
Buying automobiles, 37–38

Cabbage chowder recipe, 59
Cadnam, England, 83
Caernarvon Castle, Wales, 97
Cambridge, England, 89, 99, 100–102
Camping carnets, 31, 65
Campsites, 41–45
    amenities, 43
    fees, 64–65, 79
    guides to, 42, 44–45
    inflation, avoiding, 64–65
    location, 42
    seasons and holidays, 43
Campsites in Europe, 44
Campsite stew recipe, 52

Canal boating, 160–161
Canned goods, 46, 47, 49
Cannes, France, 140
Capel Curig, Wales, 96
Capri, Isle of, 146–147
Caravan Club Foreign Touring Handbook,
    44
Caravan rental, 38
Car Ferry Enquiries, Ltd., 39
Carnets, 31, 65
Cassington, England, 87, 92
Castellammare di Stabia, Italy, 146
Cavendish, England, 102
Chairs, 25
Châlon-sur-Saone, France, 137
Chambéry, France, 139
Chantilly, France, 135, 137
Charter flights, 14
Cheddar, England, 85
Cheese bisque recipe, 59
Cheese fondue recipe, 53
Cheese rarebit recipe, 53
Chester, England, 89, 97
Chichester, England, 77, 81
Chicken curry recipe, 53–54
Chicken with green beans recipe, 54
Chipping Norton, England, 87
Clothing, 18–21
Coq au vin recipe, 54
Collecting, 71
Cologne, Germany, 155–156
Colwyn Bay, Wales, 97
Compulsiveness, 73
Comrie, Scotland, 108
Coniston, England, 98
Consumer Guide to International Air
    Travel, 68
Consumer Guide to Air Charters, 15
Conversion tables, 171–173
Cooking, see Food
Coolers, 49
Copenhagen, Denmark, 27, 117–118, 128
Corn chowder recipe, 60
Corned beef boiled dinner recipe, 54–55
Corned beef hash with eggs recipe, 55
Cortina, Italy, 152, 158
Cost estimate, 11–13, 66–67

Côte d'Azur, 140
Cotswolds, England, 77, 88
Cowes, England, 82, 83
Crab bisque recipe, 60
Crab cakes recipe, 58
Crathie, Scotland, 106, 109
Credit cards, 11–12
Croyde, England, 85
Cully, Switzerland, 137
Customs, 14
Customs Hints for Returning U.S. Residents, 14

Dartmoor, England, 77
Dartmouth, England, 84
Dehydrated foods, 49
Denmark, 114, 116–118, 127–128, 165
Devizes, England, 86
Devon, England, 85
Dijon, France, 137
Dinkelsbühl, Germany, 154
Dinner recipes, 50–63
Dole, France, 137
Dolgellau, Wales, 95, 96
Dorchester, England, 83
Dorking, England, 81
Dornie, Scotland, 110
Doune Castle, Scotland, 113
Druid, Wales, 95
Duffel bags, 21
Dundee, Scotland, 108
Dungeon Castle, Scotland, 111
Dunkeld, Scotland, 109
Dunster, England, 85

Eating, see Food
Edam, Holland, 134
Edinburgh, Scotland, 106–108
Eidfjord, Norway, 125
Elgin, Scotland, 110
Ely, England, 102
Emergencies, 67–70
    bumping on airlines, 68
    medical problems, 69
    passports, loss of, 68
    traffic laws, 69–70
    traveler's checks, loss of, 68–69

England, 160, 161, 165–166
    central circuit, 89–103
    southwestern circuit, 77–88
Equipment, 22–28
    buying abroad, 26–27
    for children, 28
    list of, 22–24
    renting, 24, 26
Estimating costs, 11–13, 66–67
Europa Camping and Caravaning, 45
Europe, itineraries for, 130–156
Exeter, England, 77, 83, 84–85
Exmoor, England, 85
Extensions, tent, 25–26

Fagernes, Norway, 124
Ferrara, Italy, 149
Ferry transportation, 39
Ffestiniog, Wales, 95, 96
Fiesole, Italy, 141
Findhorn, Scotland, 10
Finland, 114
Fires, 48
Fishbourne, England, 81
Flam, Norway, 125
Florence, Italy, 140, 141–143
Fontainebleau, France, 135, 137
Food, 45–64
    beverages, 46–47, 49
    cooking, 46
    costs, 62–64, 79
    local suggestions, 164–170
    sample menu plans and recipes, 48–64
Fort William, Scotland, 106, 111, 112
France, 135–137, 139, 140, 161, 166–167
Fraserburgh, Scotland, 108
Freeze-dried foods, 49
Fruit, 49
Fyn, Denmark, 128

Garmisch-Partenkirchen, Germany, 153, 154
Gasoline coupons, 38, 66
Gaupne, Norway, 124
Geneva, Switzerland, 137–138
Genoa, Italy, 140
Germany, 153–156, 167

Ghent, Belgium, 135
Giethoorn, Holland, 134
Glencoe, Scotland, 112
Gotland, Sweden, 119
Grasmere, England, 98, 99
Grenoble, France, 139
Gudvangen, Norway, 125
Guides, campsite, 42, 44–45
Guildford, England, 82

Haddington, Scotland, 108
Hafelekar, Austria, 152
Hälsingborg, Sweden, 118, 119
Ham with potato patties recipe, 55
Hapsford, England, 97
Harrogate, England, 99
Haugesund, Norway, 126
Hawaiian chicken recipe, 54
Hayling Island, England, 82
Heidelberg, Germany, 154–155
Heilbronn, Germany, 154
Helsingør (Elsinore), Denmark, 118
Henley, England, 88, 92
Hindhead, England, 82
Historic Houses, Castles, and Gardens, 80
Holidays, 43
Holland, 132–133, 159–160, 161, 168–169
Holyrood Abbey, Scotland, 107–108
Holyrood Palace, Scotland, 107
Home exchange, 32–36
Hönefuss, Norway, 124
Honiton, England, 85
Hope Cove, England, 83, 84
Horsham, England, 81
Hot dogs au gratin recipe, 56
Hot dogs/baked beans recipe, 56
Hot dogs/sauerkraut recipe, 57
Houseboats, 160–161
Householding, 32–36
Höyheimsvik, Norway, 124
Huntington, England, 99

Iceland, 114
Igls, Austria, 152
Ijsselmeer, Holland, 134
Ilfracombe, England, 85

Innsbruck, Austria, 152
Insurance, purchasing, 13
International driving permit, 38
Inverbervie, Scotland, 108
Invergarry, Scotland, 111
Invermoriston, Scotland, 110
Inverness, Scotland, 106, 109–110
Isle of Skye, Scotland, 111
Isle of Wight, England, 77, 82, 83
Italian lakes, 138–140
Italian Riviera, 140
Italy, 65, 66, 139–152, 158, 167–168
Itineraries, 9–10, 75–156
   Central Europe, 130–156
   England (central circuit), 89–103
   England (southwestern circuit), 77–88
   Scandinavia, 114–129
   Scotland, 104–113
Ivrea, Italy, 139

Jönköping, Sweden, 119
Jostedal, Norway, 124
Journals, 71

Kalam, Sweden, 119
Kalmar, Sweden, 118–119
Kendal, England, 97, 99
Karlstad, Sweden, 122
Kaupanger, Norway, 124
Kenilworth, England, 95
Kenmore, Scotland, 109
Kessock, Scotland, 110
Keswick, England, 98, 99
Kidderminster, England, 95
Kidlington, England, 87, 92
Kinghorn, Scotland, 108
Kingsbridge, England, 83, 84
Kinlochleven, Scotland, 112
Kinross, Scotland, 108
Kinsarvik, Norway, 125, 126
Kirkcaldy, Scotland, 108
Klampenborg, Denmark, 118
Koblenz, Germany, 155
Korsør, Denmark, 128
Kristiansand, Norway, 127
Kristianstad, Sweden, 118

Kroken, Norway, 124
Kvanndal, Norway, 125, 126
Kyle of Lochalsh, Scotland, 110

La Croix-s-Lutry, Switzerland, 137
Ladby, Denmark, 128
Laerdal, Norway, 124
Lake District, England, 97–99, 103
Lancaster, England, 97
Lanterns, 25
La Spézié, Italy, 140
Lausanne, Switzerland, 137
Lavenham, England, 102
Leasing automobiles, 38
Lech, Austria, 150–159
Lechlade, England, 87
Leeds, England, 99
Leith Hill, England, 81
Lerici, Italy, 140
Lidingö, Sweden, 121
Lido, Italy, 151
Lisse, Holland, 134
Little Compton, England, 87
Llanberis, Wales, 96–97
Llandrillo, Wales, 95
Llangollen, Wales, 95
Llydaw, Wales, 96
Loch Ness, Scotland, 110
Loen, Norway, 124
Lofthus, Norway, 125
Lom, Norway, 124
London, England, 26–27, 102
Lossiemouth, Scotland, 110
Lucca, Italy, 144
Luggage, 17–18, 21
Luster, Norway, 124
Lyme Regis, England, 83
Lymington, England, 83
Lyngby, Denmark, 118
Lyon, France, 137

Maggiore, Italy, 147
Maidenhead, England, 88
Maiori, Italy, 147
Malmö, Sweden, 118
Manchester, England, 161

Mannheim, Germany, 155
Maps, 9
Marken, Holland, 134
Marseilles, France, 140
Massalubrense, Italy, 146
Medical problems, 69
Menus, sample, 48–64
Mestre, Italy, 149
Mies, Switzerland, 137
Milan, Italy, 139, 140
Mileage charts, sample, 9–10
Minore, Italy, 147
Monnickendam, Holland, 134
Monte Carlo, 140
Montreaux, Switzerland, 138
Moresgaard, Denmark, 128
Moreton-in-Marsh, England, 87
Morges, Switzerland, 137
Munich, Germany, 154
Murano, Italy, 151
Mutters, Austria, 152

Nairn, Scotland, 110
Newbridge, Scotland, 108
Nice, France, 140
Nigardsbre, Norway, 124
Nigg, Scotland, 108
Norrköping, Sweden, 119
Northleach, England, 87
Norway, 114, 116, 122–127, 169
Norwich, England, 161
Nyborg, Denmark, 128
Nyon, Switzerland, 137, 138

Oban, Scotland, 106, 112
Odense, Denmark, 128
Okehampton, England, 85
Öland, Sweden, 119
Oriental seafood recipe, 58
Orkney Islands, Scotland, 111
Oslo, Norway, 122–124
Ostia, Italy, 144
Ovre, Norway, 125
Oxford, England, 79, 87, 89, 91–92

Packing list, 18–21
Padua, Italy, 149
Paella recipe, 57–58
Paestum, Italy, 147–148
Paris, France, 135–137
Passports, 14, 65, 68
Patscherkofel, Austria, 152
Penrhyndeudraeth, Wales, 95, 96
Perishable foods, 46
Perugia, Italy, 144
Peterborough, England, 102
Peterhead, Scotland, 108
Petworth, England, 82
Pisa, Italy, 140, 141, 143
Pitlochry, Scotland, 106, 109
Plymouth, England, 84, 85
Poligny, France, 137
Pompeii, Italy, 148
Poole, England, 83
Portofino, Italy, 140
Portree, Scotland, 111
Portsmouth, England, 82
Positano, Italy, 147
Praiano, Italy, 147

Randers, Denmark, 127
Ravello, Italy, 147
Ravenna, Italy, 149
Recipes, 50–62
Relaxation, 73–74
Renting:
    automobiles, 36–38
    caravans, 38
    equipment, 24, 26
Revsnes, Norway, 124
Rice recipe, 57
Rimini, Italy, 149
Ringöy, Norway, 125
Roldal, Norway, 126
Rome, Italy, 144–146, 149
Rothenburg ob der Tauber, Germany, 154
Routes, see Itineraries
Royston, England, 102
Rydal, England, 98
Ryde, England, 82

Saffron Walden, England, 102
St. Andrews, Scotland, 106, 108
Salcombe, England, 77, 83, 84
Salerno, Italy, 147
Salisbury, England, 77, 95
Saltsjöbaden, Sweden, 121
Salzburg, Austria, 153
San Candido, Italy, 152
Sandhamn, Sweden, 121
Sandnes, Norway, 126
Sandown, England, 82
San Gimignano, Italy, 144
San Remo, Italy, 140
Sauda, Norway, 126
Sausages/cabbage recipe, 57
Scammadale, Scotland, 112
Scandinavia, 114–129
Schools, 35
Scotland, 104–113, 160
Seafood chowder recipe, 60
Seasons, 43
Sea travel, 16–18
Seefelt, Austria, 152
Seegrube, Austria, 152
Sherried ham recipe, 55
Shipping automobiles, 39
Shipping lines, 17
Shrewsbury, England, 95
Siena, Italy, 143
Sightseeing, 66, 70, 72–73
Skare, Norway, 126
Skiing, 157–159
Skillet tuna recipe, 58
Skipton, England, 99
Skjolden, Norway, 124
Skudeneshaven, Norway, 126
Sleeping bags, 24
Sligachan, Scotland, 111
Sloppy Joes recipe, 52
Sogndal, Norway, 124
Sognefjord area, Norway, 124–125
Sorrento, Italy, 146, 147
Soups, 59–61
Spaghetti and meatballs recipe, 52
Spakenburg, Holland, 134

Spam and macaroni recipe, 56
Spam Spanish rice recipe, 56
Spam with olives recipe, 56
Spanish rice recipe, 52–53
Spean Bridge, Scotland, 111
Spoleto, Italy, 144
Sports, 72
Staphorst, Holland, 134
Stavanger, Norway, 126–127
Stirling, Scotland, 113
Stockholm, Sweden, 119–121
Stonehaven, Scotland, 108
Stonehenge, England, 77, 86
Stoves, 24, 48–49
Stow-on-the-Wold, England, 87
Stratford-upon-Avon, England, 89, 93–94,
    161
Stresa, Italy, 138, 139
Studley, England, 95
Sweden, 114, 116, 118–122, 169–170
Swindon, England, 87
Switzerland, 137–138, 157–159, 160, 170

Tables, 25
Tannay, Switzerland, 137
Tents, 24–26
Tmorne, England, 99
Tivoli, Italy, 144
Tobermory, Scotland, 112
Torcello, Italy, 151
Torino, Italy, 139
Tourist information, 28–30
Traffic laws, 69–70
Traveler's checks, 68–69
Trawsfynydd, Wales, 95, 96
Trondheim, Norway, 127
Trumpington, England, 102
Tuna oriental recipe, 59
Tyndrum, Scotland, 113

Ugborough, England, 83
Uitdam, Holland, 134

Uppsala, Sweden, 121–122
Utrecht, Holland, 135, 156

Vaccinations, 14
Vangsnes, Norway, 124
Värmland, Sweden, 122
Vatican City, Italy, 145–146
Vegetables, 49, 61–62
Venice, Italy, 149–152
Verbier, Switzerland, 159
Verona, Italy, 152
Versailles, France, 135, 137
Vesenaz, Switzerland, 137
Vettica, Italy, 147
Vietri, Italy, 147
Viksdalen, Norway, 124
Visas, 14
Visby, Sweden, 119
Volendam, Holland, 134
Vittoria Veneto, Italy, 152
Voss, Norway, 125

Wallingford, England, 87, 88, 92
Wareham, England, 83
Warwick, England, 94–95
Weather, 25, 67
Welsh soup recipe, 60
Whedden Cross, England, 85
Winchester, England, 77
Windermere, England, 97, 98
Windsor Castle, England, 88, 91–92
Wines, 46
Woodstock, England, 93
Worms, Germany, 155
Worthing, England, 81

Yarmouth, England, 83, 161
York, England, 99
Ystad, Sweden, 118–119

Zermatt, Switzerland, 159